THE PROFESSIONAL SINGER'S HANDBOOK

by Gloria Rusch

HAL•LEONARD® CORPORATION

7777 W. BLUEMOUND RD. P.O. BOX 13819 MILWAUKEE, WI 53213

Visit Hal Leonard Online at
www.halleonard.com

Grateful acknowledgment is made to John Novello and to Alma Caesari-Gramatke and Rolf Gramatke for permission to reprint selections from their copyrighted works.

COVER: Gloria Rusch in concert
PHOTO By Joan Tourtellot

EDITED by Daveda Lamont
COVER DESIGN by Gloria Rusch, Marc Fett and Rachel Rausch
COMPUTER GRAPHIC ILLUSTRATIONS by Rod Altschull
DIGITAL LAYOUT, IMAGING & PREPRESS by Randy Tobin at Theta Data

ACKNOWLEDGMENTS

I would like to express my sincere thanks to Daveda Lamont for working with me through the entire creation of this work and whose superb editing helped transform my manuscript into a fully realized and flowing communication; my husband John for his love, wisdom, experience, advice, encouragement, understanding and support; my daughters Rachel and Ileane for their love and support; a special thanks to Ileane and Alissa Haggis for helping me with the transcriptions; Marc Fett for his dedication, hard work, support and friendship; Geoff Levin for his generous assistance; Izzy and Maryann Chait for their friendship and support; my friend, the late Laura Hippe, for recommending that I go to The School of the Natural Voice, where my first teacher, David Kaufman, introduced me to The Old Italian School of Singing and the Caesari technology that saved my voice; Nancy West, one of the voice teachers who worked with me at the School; Marco for his friendship and being an incredible trainer during our workouts; my mom and dad, Dorothy and Neal, who always had music playing around the house, paid for my first music lessons and encouraged my artistic abilities; my sister Marguerite and late sister Brenda for the wonderful vocal harmonies we sang while washing dishes; my brother Neal and Kenny and late brother Michael for their artistic talent, love and support.

I would also like to express my very deep appreciation to all the great artists who took off valuable time from their busy schedules to share their insight and expertise in their interviews; to students everywhere whose quest for vocal knowledge and improvement actually inspired this work. A very special thanks to the staff at Celebrity Centre® International and L. Ron Hubbard, whose technology on life and livingness is priceless.

To Dorothy and Neal Sr., John,

Rachel, Ileane, Sparky and Odin

CONTENTS

PREFACE

I chose to write this book after realizing that most of the people coming to me for private voice coaching want more than breathing exercises, scales and work on songs, and that there are many questions that beginning singers and vocalists have in common. Time and time again I have been asked questions such as *How do I know if I have the talent to become a singer? When should I get a manager? How do I get a record deal?* I have frequently found myself spending almost an entire lesson giving career counseling.

In my own quest for knowledge on "making it" in the music industry and the things a singer needs to know beyond scales and singing songs, I discovered there wasn't a book available that would teach it to me, even though there are thousands of books on vocal technique, the business of music publishing, getting a record deal and so on. Singers are probably the only group of musicians who have to learn everything almost exclusively from cold, hard experience and the school of hard knocks!

And so I have learned through my own experiences as a professional singer/songwriter and actress a great deal about what an up-and-coming singer needs to know to be prepared for the long bumpy road ahead. My goal in writing this book is to shine some light on what to expect in various situations a singer might find himself or herself in, and give him/her some idea of how to handle them. I want to give singers a realistic idea of what they can expect from working with managers, other singers, musicians, sound techs, producers, songwriters, record company execs and owners.

Even if you've been in the music business awhile and have some knowledge of the business, the information contained in these pages may help you achieve your goals faster. There just might be that one piece of advice you never thought of—how to handle a group member, a manager, or sound person you're working with; how to conquer stage fright; what to expect with studio and session work.

This information has proven extremely valuable to many. As a matter of fact, many of the students who have seriously applied it to their own careers have gone on to sign record deals, star in Broadway shows, and become successful singer/songwriters and session singers. And some who didn't have the dream of fame and fortune, but just wanted to overcome their stage fright and sing for their own pleasure or for their friends and family, have become happy with having developed knowledge to enhance that ability.

The road to success is littered with forgotten dreams and the failed attempts of so many artists who reached for the stars. I hope this books helps you to keep your dreams alive and make them come true. Be persistent and go for it!

Best wishes,

Gloria Rusch

INTRODUCTORY NOTE

Keep in mind as you read this book that there are never two situations that are exactly the same—what I have written is what I have found to be workable for myself and the people I have interviewed. Take this information and apply it to your own situation and life experiences as you seek to achieve your goal in the music industry. The exercises and drills found in this book are workable and very effective and will increase your abilities as a singer if you use them. They will help you to be prepared for any situation and deliver a dynamite performance when called upon to do so.

Chapter 1

Getting Started!

WHO IS THIS BOOK FOR?

Have you ever asked yourself questions such as these?

"Everybody says I have a great voice, but that doesn't mean I can sing for a living, does it?"

"Everybody tells me to stop when I sing along with the radio—but I really love singing! What can I do?"

Or, if you already have decided to pursue a career as a singer, you may have wanted the answers to questions like these:

"What kind of voice do I have?"

"How do I select a vocal coach?"

"What do I do once I become a STAR?"

Well, with the information contained in this book, no matter whether you're already singing or not, I hope to answer these questions and many others without the negative feedback you all too frequently get when you tell someone about your dream. Over many years of teaching I've learned that most singers have the same concerns. I've worked with complete beginners as well as multi-platinum recording artists, and they all have to walk the same path, no matter what kind of music they sing.

Throughout the book, definitions and explanations of various music terms are provided in parentheses. A Glossary of Studio Terms appears at the end of Chapter 7, and a Bibliography of recommended reading appears at the end of the book.

So let's begin!

CAN I SING?

Everyone, except for those born without any vocal cords, can sing. Remember when you were a kid and you would run around the house or playground or sit in a room playing with your toys, and you hummed a simple little tune? Remember when you used to sing your favorite nursery rhymes with your friends or a parent or grandparent? All of that was and still is singing ... don't let anyone tell you any different!

"Well," you say, "if that was singing, what happened? Why can't I sing in tune? Why am I tone deaf? I couldn't sing a note now if my life depended on it!"

In my experience with hundreds of students, I have found that every singer who made one of those statements to me had had a bad experience early in his or her life concerning their singing. Usually it was with a singing teacher, a parent or close friend. It may even have occurred when they were already singing, but were made to feel really bad about their performance. Right afterward, they came to some sort of conclusion or decision based on the bad experience. They may have decided that they couldn't sing or that they would never sing again. As a result of that decision, the singer never got past that horrible incident and their decision stayed with them forever—or until they somehow gathered enough courage to try again. But often only the most determined are able to get back out there, try again, and risk loss after loss as they put themselves on the line to go for the big time—a career as a professional singer.

If *you* had an experience like this at some point in your life, you should first realize that *any* singing problem can be corrected. That's right, *any* problem! Thus, any idea you may have gotten that you can never be a good singer is simply not true. All you actually need is the willingness to go after your dream, and the information to help you get there. That's what this book is all about.

DO I HAVE THE *TALENT* TO BECOME A PROFESSIONAL?

The word "talent" is thrown around in the entertainment field so frequently that it has acquired a near-mystical connotation, as though talent were an indefinable quality that only certain people are blessed with. We know when an artist we are watching *has* it, but not many people seem to know how you *get* it, or even what it really means.

The *Macmillan Dictionary for Students* defines "talent" as "special aptitude or ability." The *Oxford American Dictionary* defines it as "special or very great ability." From these definitions we see that talent boils down to *ability*. And although the word *ability* can be used to describe the overall ability that an accomplished artist demonstrates, any good singer's total performance arises out of that artist's use of *many* skills and abilities. Some of these abilities may be natural, but by far the greatest number of them have been developed through learning, practice, hard work, the will to succeed and persistence. And these skills and abilities include not only those things that are directly related to the act of singing itself, but also things like the ability to communicate with an audience, stage presence, the ability to choose the right music and songs, the ability to choose the right group to back you up, belief in yourself, and the ability to rise above disappointments.

For these reasons, a question like "Do I have the talent to become a professional?" can be misleading, because rather than talent being a make-or-break proposition—either you have it or you don't—there are many, many factors that you *can* control that will determine the answer. And, in fact, probably the most important abilities anyone can have are the will to succeed and unfailing persistence in going after their dreams. I'm sure you can think of many superstars whose voices are unusual or imperfect in some way. They became stars anyway because of their strong will to succeed and their desire to really connect with their audiences with powerful emotions.

There is another way that someone might be misled into thinking they don't have the talent to succeed. Say you want to become a professional singer and have been trying to sing rock & roll. After experimenting around with it for a while, you still don't feel great about how your voice sounds. You don't know what's wrong, and you start to think you might not have the talent to make your career happen.

Then one day, just for the hell of it, you try a country song—and suddenly you find magic! You realize that what that was wrong before was not that you didn't have talent, but that rock & roll wasn't the right style of music for your voice. By taking a chance, you found what I call "your heart" as a singer! You found out you have plenty of talent as a country singer! Therefore, doing research into the style that best suits you and your voice is a very important responsibility. Sometimes it can even take years. But when you find what's right for you, it's magical and well worth the effort. So don't be afraid to experiment and try singing the kind of music you always *really*, secretly, wanted to sing!

HOW TECHNICALLY PROFICIENT DO I HAVE TO BE?

You don't have to be a great technician to become a professional singer. But it's always better to be in command of your basics as a vocalist. And you will find that in the finer arts of singing, such as classical and opera, more attention is put on technical perfection than in other styles.

Be your own judge and listen to singers in each basic style of music—opera and classical, musical theater, pop, jazz, blues, R&B (rhythm and blues), country, rock, heavy metal, and all the other forms in between, and you'll find out which styles demand more technical expertise and which demand less. Some forms actually require that you have a great deal of expertise both in your technical singing ability and as a communicator. "Communication?" you ask. Yes, communication is not only important, but *vital* when singing. I'll get into the subject of communication a little later in this book.

So get your hands on CD's or cassettes of the styles of music you like and sing along with them. This is a good way to discover the style of music that best suits you and your voice. If you're on a tight budget, some libraries carry CD's you can borrow. By the way, if you have a choice between buying or making a copy of a friend's CD, go ahead and buy it. Remember, every time you make a copy of a CD, you're cheating the artist out of his or her hard-earned money. Someday you could be the artist who gets cheated, and I'm sure you have heard of the expression, "What goes around comes around"!

DO I HAVE WHAT IT TAKES TO BECOME A PROFESSIONAL SINGER?

Well, let's see. What's a professional singer? To answer this question you first have to know what a professional is. Lots of people use the word without the slightest idea what it means!

The dictionary says a *professional* is "a person who earns a living in a sport or other occupation frequently engaged in by amateurs" (*Random House Electronic Dictionary*). That was always my understanding—if you earned a living at something, you could call yourself a professional. But this is definitely not all there is to it.

The dictionary also says a *professional* is "a person who is expert at his or her work" (*Random House Electronic Dictionary*). Now we're getting closer to a meaning that can help you. If you are an expert singer, you stand a much better chance of winning over audiences and having plenty of work.

But there's more to it than even that. I learned what it really means to be a professional after working in the business as both an actress and a singer. When I began my first acting class with Robert F. Lyons he said, "When you walk into this classroom you are considered a professional. I expect you to behave in a professional manner at all times. Show up on time and do your work."

Show Up On Time. Yes, one of the first things a real professional does is show up on time for appointments, rehearsals, recording sessions, performances, and yes, even voice lessons. If a singer can't show up on time for a lesson, how is he or she ever going to make it in the business? The vocal coach or teacher is one of the first people who is actually going to help you improve your craft so you can achieve your goal as a singer, no matter what that goal is. He or she could be a very important person in the development of your blossoming career and should be treated with the same respect you'd expect to be treated yourself.

Do your homework. In my opinion, this is one of *the* most important things a professional does—*practice!* Basketball great Michael Jordan said practice is the only way for anyone to achieve his level of skill. In singing you get good by singing, you do it by singing and carrying out all the assignments given to you by your instructor, producer, or whoever is working with you.

Always Do the Best Job You Can, and Give More Than Anybody Expects. Never, ever do anything partway or glibly (superficially or insincerely). If you feel you need help, don't be ashamed to ask for it. And there is another quality that distinguishes true professionals and makes them stand out as exceptional artists. They go *beyond* just "doing the work"—they work harder than they have to. In other words, they give *way more* than anybody expects! As a result, they present a brilliant piece of work. And this is the secret of how an artist actually becomes brilliant. So give your all!

Have a professional attitude toward your work, the people you work with, and yourself. You sometimes hear about artists in the business who make lots of money and sell lots of records, but are late or irresponsible in their business dealings. Others are tyrannical, temperamental and difficult to work with. Believe me, eventually all this catches up with them. These artists lose respect as their reputation of being unprofessional gets around the industry. They start losing their business and job offers and as a result, their credibility. Their income diminishes, and it just gets worse from there. One opera singer I heard about earned herself this kind of reputation. As a result, none of the repertory opera companies in the United States were willing to hire her.

To sum up, having a professional attitude means honoring your commitments and being responsible (able to be trusted and depended upon; willing to control and take care of things), both in your business dealings and in your relations with everyone you work with. A professional is someone who demonstrates their responsibility by showing up on time and doing their work. He or she is sincere and dedicated to their profession and goals. And in addition to this, professionals are known as exceptional artists because they always go above and beyond the usual or expected in their work—they deliver an outstanding product!

Now that you know what it takes to be a professional singer, you will be better able to judge whether or not you *have* what it takes. As you begin to work toward your goals and get a feel for it, you will gain a better idea of whether this career is for you or not. You may find out you don't like to put in the long hours it takes to become a professional, or you don't like the lifestyle or pressure. On the other hand, you may thrive on it—this is what you always wanted!

EXERCISES

1. Have you ever been made fun of or invalidated when you sang, and afterwards felt like backing off from singing or stopping entirely? If so, take a sheet of paper and write down what happened each time.

2. Make a list of artists you feel are exceptionally talented. Do a little research on each of the artists you named and find out what they did to help develop their talent and ultimately their career. You can sometimes find interviews in magazines or on the Internet.

3. Take an honest look at the songs you are singing and decide if they are really the kind of songs you love to sing and if they are suited for your voice. Don't be afraid to try another style. Make a simple recording of yourself singing the different songs and listen to them. Decide which song sounds better and communicates well to the listener.

4. Write down some examples of when you were unprofessional.

5. Write down some examples of when you delivered an exceptional piece of work.

CHAPTER 2

HOW TO SELECT A VOCAL COACH

So now you have some songs to sing and you find you're not able to control your voice and make it do the things you want it to. Or, while listening to your CD's or to other singers, you hear things you want your voice to do, but don't know how to achieve them. The next step is to take some voice lessons.

This chapter will guide you in selecting the vocal coach best suited to your needs and steer you away from mistakes and pitfalls that can not only be costly, but sometimes harmful to your voice as well.

HOW DO I KNOW IF I NEED A VOCAL COACH?

First of all, who needs a voice teacher or vocal coach? Anyone who is seeking knowledge about the voice and how it operates. Anyone who wishes to improve his or her vocal abilities, be it range, interpretation skills, ability to hear pitches, or communication skills. Anyone who feels they've outgrown their current voice teacher. In short, anyone who wants to improve or repair their voice, or just plain wants to sing better.

If you've ever been told you are tone deaf, you are also a prime candidate for voice lessons—but be cautious, for this is one of several basic misconceptions in the business that are forwarded by teachers. Factually, THERE IS NO SUCH THING AS A TONE DEAF SINGER. Yes, you heard me right! There is no such thing—merely one who is not hearing and distinguishing pitches well. A good teacher can train someone to hear the notes correctly through use of the right scales and technique.

So now you've read all the voice instruction ads in the different trade magazines. Maybe a friend has recommended a coach or perhaps you've already started shopping around, trying a lesson here and another there. But you weren't happy with the results or the vibes just weren't right. You want to be sure, because your choice can make—or break—your career. How are you ever going to discover who is the best teacher for your particular needs?

I have found on many occasions that when a student calls me to inquire about voice lessons, he or she doesn't know what to ask other than what the price is and where my studio is located. But there are a number of things you should know before you make your decision.

Of course a big concern is bucks. How much is it going to cost? Lessons can range from $20 to $250 an hour. As with any product, let the buyer beware! It's possible you may be paying for a *name* and not much more, if you choose the most expensive. On the other hand, the cheapest lessons might be more expensive than you would ever think, because you could pay with the loss of your voice if you receive incorrect technique. Don't let the price be the sole determining factor for you. The following information should assist you in making an informed and knowing choice so you don't have to take a shot in the dark and come up losing.

A good vocal coach will know and teach all aspects of singing you need to be successful. The bottom line in any singing is being able to relax and open up. A teacher should work toward this and thoroughly cover such things as singing technique (and there is much more to technique than just scales), communication, diet as it relates to voice, and the effects of smoking and drugs on the singer.

VOCAL TECHNIQUES

I don't believe in using any vocal technique that requires you to do unnatural things such as bending over to hit a high note, raising your upper lip over your teeth and frowning to sing high notes, forcing your ribs to go one way while your butt goes another, or pinching your butt to produce a note! I don't make funny animal sounds or give people the "raspberries" when I sing, either. It's just common sense. I never sing that way onstage or in the studio, so what's the point of using those types of things as a vocal technique? I've tried them all, and I never found any of them useful. One teacher in Los Angeles actually uses a car buffer (polisher) and a chain saw on his students—*and* charges them $1,500.00 per hour to do it! Now, *that* one I've never tried—and I don't plan to!

What I have discovered is that these odd "techniques" or "tricks" are actually unusual and improper "solutions" that are used to try to remedy an inadequate vocal technique. In other words, these improper solutions are dreamed up when the vocal technique being used can't actually produce the correct result!

Have the teacher sing for you. He or she is the best example of the singing technique being used. Be aware, however, that there are many teachers who are great singers but can't teach what they know to another person.

COMMUNICATION

Singing not only involve the details of technique like pitch, rhythm, and phrasing, although some teachers will take up all the student's time and attention with these aspects. Rather, singing has everything to do with communication. This mainly involves two things: the message you are trying to get across, and the emotion of the song. It's the teacher's responsibility to see that the student understands this and to help the student achieve the ability to communicate powerfully through his or her singing.

And while we're on the subject of communication, students need to select a teacher they can communicate with freely. A student should feel comfortable and safe not only in singing for the teacher, but in saying what they think! Your interview with prospective teachers is your chance to observe their communication skills and how well they communicate with you.

Ask the prospective teacher why he/she decided to become a teacher. How this question is answered will tell you the kind of attention and care your voice will receive. If he's just doing it to make money until he can do something else, you may not want to entrust your voice to him. Ask if he is still performing and if not, why he stopped. If he is teaching because he couldn't make it as a singer, you shouldn't be studying with him. Such a teacher may be passing along his own confusions and failures as a vocalist.

A good teacher should always treat his students with respect. As a teacher, I never invalidate or put down students when they make an error or miss while attempting to do something correctly. There are ways of guiding a student without making him/her feel small or bad. The teacher should acknowledge a student for something he/she did right before telling him/her how they can improve. This is very important. Above all, a teacher should never *ever* make a student look bad in front of another student—or anyone, for that matter. Nothing can be gained from that type of teaching other than making the student feel very uncomfortable and introverting him/her. Sometimes it can make him/her give up singing altogether.

A good vocal coach should also always be willing to learn from his students. Each student is unique and has his/her own special qualities and abilities. A good teacher is one who can observe the student in front of him and understand his/her particular goals, needs and problems.

ARE OTHER STUDENTS SATISFIED?

Locate and ask singers who have studied with the coach what they got out of the lessons and if and how their voices improved. Be very sure to ask honest, direct questions.

If the teacher is promoting *who* he teaches as one of his selling points, go and listen to those singers. Many *stars* have great voices prior to studying with a teacher, yet the teacher takes credit for making the star a successful singer when in fact the star may have had just a few lessons. If you can, talk to the singers and ask them how they like the teacher, how long they've been studying with him, how the teacher has improved their voices and if they are happy with the results they are getting with the technique. Note *when* that teacher taught them as well as the longevity of the singer. If you like their answers, and if those answers are representative of the direction you want to go in, then that teacher may be the correct coach for you.

THE NATURAL SINGER

A teacher might get lucky and get a student who is a natural singer to start with. E. Herbert-Caesari, in Chapter III of his book *Tradition and Gigli* [1] defined the natural voice as follows:

> The completely natural voice is one which sings effortlessly on all vowels perfectly, with great ease across its entire range. We see no strain anywhere, no trembling of a distorted mouth opening, no inexpressive frowning indicative of strain and anxiety, no "cordy" neck, no red face performances. Summing up, therefore, THE COMPLETELY NATURAL VOICE REFLECTS THE TRUTH OF VOCAL TECHNIQUE AND PRODUCTION, and by faithfully obeying physiological and acoustical laws as applied to the voice, reveals them with the utmost clarity—to those sufficiently circumspect.

A natural singer can be a gem to a teacher who recognizes his or her natural abilities. A teacher who is instructing such a singer should only enhance what the natural student is already doing and educate that singer to his or her natural abilities.

HOW WILL I KNOW IF THE VOICE LESSONS ARE WORKING?

If you're studying with a vocal coach and you've been honestly doing your homework and practicing, you should start to see very good results in about three months.

---

1   Excerpted with permission from Alma Caesari-Gramatke, from *Tradition and Gigli*, by E. Herbert-Caesari, copyright by Alma and Rolf Gramatke, London NW6 7QS, 41 Mowbray Road.

However, when you start your lessons, if the data the teacher is giving you can't be directly applied to your singing to improve it—if you can't *use* it—then you should question its validity or the credibility of the teacher giving it. The teacher may not actually understand how the data works. If your voice has not improved, or has gotten worse since you started to study, then there is obviously something wrong with the teacher or the technique being taught.

Additionally, if you had the ability to sing well prior to taking voice lessons, but begin to lose that ability and control after working with a teacher, that teacher is using a technique that will ultimately destroy your voice. Sometimes this destructive process may take years. However, starting to lose your voice is one of the first signs of incorrect technique. Other signs include the throat and neck muscles starting to hurt and/or being tight and strained. You may become unable to reach notes you want to, and may find you've lost your speaking voice after a gig. The extreme example would be developing nodes (calluses) on the vocal cords.

By the way, nodes on the vocal cords as a result of incorrect vocal technique do not necessarily mean surgery. See the section "How to Handle Vocal Nodes."in Chapter 5, "Staying Healthy and Sane."

THE STUDENT'S RESPONSIBILITIES

We've covered the responsibilities of the vocal coach. But what about the student's responsibilities to the teacher? Here are some tips to assist you in maintaining a good relationship with your coach.

First, show up for your lessons on time and ready to work. That includes being well-rested and fed. Call if you're going to be late or if you can't keep your appointment. It's very upsetting to a teacher to have a student not show up for an appointment. Call and let her know if you can't make it and when you can reschedule so she will trust you next time. Failing to show up makes everyone lose—you, the teacher, and anyone else who could have used that lesson time!

Second, be willing to pay for any time you take from the teacher by not keeping your appointment—particularly if you gave too little notice for her to schedule someone else (usually 24 hours). In the long run this will pay off in keeping a good relationship with your teacher. It shows you're responsible and serious about your lessons. It also shows you care about your teacher and encourages her to care about you. She may end up giving you extra time on a lesson.

Finally, by all means practice whatever lesson plan your teacher gives you. Otherwise, you're wasting your time and money and the teacher's time. If you have any difficulties with practice—can't find the necessary time to practice, can't seem to successfully juggle your work schedule with your practice schedule, don't know how to practice, or don't have good practice discipline—see the sections "Practice Discipline" and the "Sample Practice Schedule" in Chapter 3, "The Basics of Singing."

SUMMARY - KEY QUESTIONS TO ASK THE VOCAL COACH

As you can see, there are a number of elements that all contribute to the desired result of a beneficial partnership between you and your teacher. But choosing the right one for you is the first step. To sum up, here's a list of key questions you should ask during your interview with a teacher you're considering:

1. What do the lessons cost?

2. How often should I take a lesson?

3. Where are you located?

4. What technique do you use?

5. What is your background in music?

6. Why did you become a teacher?

7. Can you help me improve my style?

8. Can I work on my own material (songs)?

9. Do you work on breathing?

10. Can you work with me in other areas like career consultation, studio singing, sight reading, song selection, ear training, etc.?

11. Do you refer me to jobs?

12. Do you recommend I warm up with vocal exercises before I start to sing songs?

13. How long do you recommend I vocalize daily?

14. Can I talk to some of the students who currently study with you?

The answers to these questions—or lack of them—will tell you a lot.

EXERCISES

1. Using the "Key Questions" in this chapter, interview a vocal coach you are thinking of studying with.

2. Choose the coach or teacher you feel most comfortable with and who in your opinion is the most qualified based on the Key Questions.

CHAPTER 3

THE BASICS OF SINGING

INTENTION AND POSTULATING YOUR NOTES

My students learn that in order to sing you first have to *postulate* what you're going to sing. In other words, *you* decide on the note, breathe, and the note follows shortly after that. That's as simple as it is... almost too simple! To postulate something means to really, clearly put it there; to make it so—to form an intention and make it reality; to have no doubts or reservations about what you've decided to do—total certainty!

So what does it mean to postulate your notes? It's simply intending to sing a note, or creating the note in your mind. It's what *you* intend and create. Some singers "see" or "hear" what they want first, then do it physically. In music and singing, you postulate all the time. You hear (postulate) the notes you want to sing an instant beforehand and your vocal cords stretch to the correct tension. When the air passes through the cords, the result is the correct note.

If the correct note doesn't come out, then you either didn't postulate it, or there is some technical problem or error that needs to be corrected. The actual fact is that poor postulating—meaning having postulates with uncertainties or negative emotions such as doubt or fear in them—is the root of all singing problems. So practicing is simply drilling your fundamentals until you feel certain enough that you can postulate again! Practice is simply a back-up to remedy imperfect postulating. Did you ever just decide to do something and then do it without practicing? Well, that's what perfect postulating is!

COMMUNICATING THE SONG

As an artist, your ability to communicate is the most important asset you have. In this section we will take a very close look at what communication actually is and how a singer should understand and use it. All throughout this book I emphasize the importance of learning the *basics* of singing. Singing in tune, having good time, good rhythm, good stage presence—all these things comprise the *technical* parts of singing and mastering them is a requirement among professional musicians and performers—there is no substitute for it. You must have *all* of your *basics*, or fundamentals, in place. So what is the relationship between technical expertise and communication? Simply this: when you add the ability to communicate to the package of basic skills, you have dynamite!

One of the first things you should know is that art is a communication. Take a look at any piece of art—a statue, a building, a painting, or even the way someone is dressed. Every one of these things is a work of art in some way, shape or form. Music and songs are also works of art. And in every instance, when you see the way the guy or girl is dressed or hear the song, a feeling or a mood or a thought is communicated to you and makes you feel a certain way. Sometimes the feeling is good and sometimes the feeling is bad. Either way it's a communication.

When you take this viewpoint of communication and apply it to yourself as a singer, it becomes a very important part of singing. I could go so far as to say it's the most senior component of your job as a singer.

When singing, you communicate both the message in the song *and* the emotion, which is how you feel about it. These two things are very close together and you can't have one without the other.

Before you can communicate the message, you have to know what you're singing about. If you don't know what you're singing about, how on earth can you deliver your message? So if you don't know what all the words in the song mean, look up their definitions. Remember, in a song you're trying to get your audience to understand what you're communicating—so *you* better understand it first!

Once you understand what you're singing about, then you have to *feel* a certain way about it. Yes, *you* have to actually *feel* something. Otherwise the audience won't believe you. The emotion you feel can be grief, anger, fear, happiness, despair, pain, and so on. When you put emotion into a song, it's like magic. It's the glue that makes everything stick together. When you listen to songs on the radio, notice that every song has some kind of emotion being communicated along with the message of the song.

Do a little experiment and see if you can figure out what emotion is being communicated in some of the songs you listen to. Consider this part of your homework or training. I'll give you a hint—usually the emotion being communicated is the one you are feeling while listening to the song.

Let's break down communication even further.

When you are onstage singing, you are communicating *to* someone. The "someone" just happens to be a room full of people. It doesn't really matter how many people are in the audience—one or 100,000. Each one of them is a person you are communicating to. Your image, the way you are dressed, your musical style, your demeanor—*all* are delivering a message to the audience. You are communicating an emotion across a distance and your audience is sitting or standing in a room listening and receiving your message. If you do a great job delivering your message (song), then they will respond with applause and cheers. The audience will let you know if you did a really good job, a mediocre job, a fantastic job, or a bad job. Deep down inside you will always know if the audience liked you, or if they were just being polite.

When the audience responds to your communication with their applause then they are letting you know they got your communication and understood it. You, in turn, should always be respectful to the audience and thank them for their acknowledgment. If you don't thank the audience, then you are being rude, disrespectful and not completing the communication you are responsible for starting in the first place.

Technical Expertise vs. Communication

One thing I must caution you about is not to put *so* much emphasis on achieving *technical perfection* with your singing that everything else falls by the wayside, including communication. If you make technical perfection your *main* goal in art, you are putting your attention on the wrong target. It *is* possible to practice and sing until you are perfect, and some musical styles demand more technical expertise than others. That's to be expected! But what I am saying is that although you should get your technical skills as a vocalist as high as possible for the type of music you are singing, you should never underestimate the importance of communicating your feelings through the song because *that* is your main goal as a singer. That is what audiences respond to more than anything else.

However, I'm not saying don't study music! In fact, the more musical training you have, the more knowledge and control you'll have with your music. I have had some singers say they don't want to take lessons because they feel they will lose the *natural thing* they have. A singer with a *natural gift* to communicate will *never* lose that natural ability simply by studying music. The only way this happens is when you put your attention on technical details as the top priority. As long as you keep the technical side in perspective, meaning you use it as a *tool* to create art with, you'll never have that problem. When you study music you broaden your horizon and knowledge in the area of music. You will learn what it is that makes you do what you do and why you have that ability. It will make it easier for you to create and write more and better songs. You will be able to improvise better and understand what other musicians and singers are doing. That isn't a bad thing, is it?

I used to play piano entirely by ear and never really knew how to read music. When I started to learn the technical side of charts (sheet music), what the symbols meant and the various technical terms, I became a better singer. My ability to communicate improved, too.

For an interesting and helpful discussion of the importance and exact role of communication in any musician's performance, I recommend you read Chapters 1 and 2 of the book, *The Contemporary Keyboardist*, by John Novello.

THE PARTS OF THE VOICE

No matter whether the singer I'm training is an experienced singer or a beginner, I see remarkable improvement in their first lesson after they learn the mechanics of the voice. This means the parts of the voice and how it really works. Imagine trying to drive a car without knowing what the gear shift lever, brake pedal, and accelerator pedal do. Or without knowing where the gas gauge and gas tank are. If you know the basic parts and functions of a car, then you can drive just about any car. In no way am I trying to say that if you don't know the parts of the voice, you won't be able to sing. But you'll sing better and have better control of your voice if you *do*.

For example, can you locate your vocal cords? Most people know they're in their throat, but where? What do they look like? How many of them are there? How do they make sound? Did you know there are 60 muscles that work the vocal cords? Did you know that 80% of the physical act of singing is breath control? Have you ever really wondered how you "sing from the diaphragm"? Every student who is trained at my school learns these very basic things.

You should know the parts of the voice including the vocal cords, the 60 muscles that work them, the larynx, soft palate, hard palate, lungs, thyroid cartilage, diaphragm, and breathing, and how all of these things interact with each other when you sing. When you know how all the parts of the voice work together, then you are able to control your voice more easily. When you have control of your voice, then you can pretty much sing whatever you want with much more ease and no strain. To learn about these mechanisms of the voice, I suggest you read *The Voice of the Mind*, by E. Herbert-Caesari and *Tradition in Gigli*, by E. Herbert-Caesari.[2]

---

2   E. Herbert-Caesari, *The Voice of the Mind*, copyright by Alma and Rolf Gramatke, London NW6 7QS, 41 Mowbray Road; *Tradition and Gigli*, copyright by Alma and Rolf Gramatke, London NW6 7QS, 41 Mowbray Road.

Vocal Cord

Thyroid Cartilage

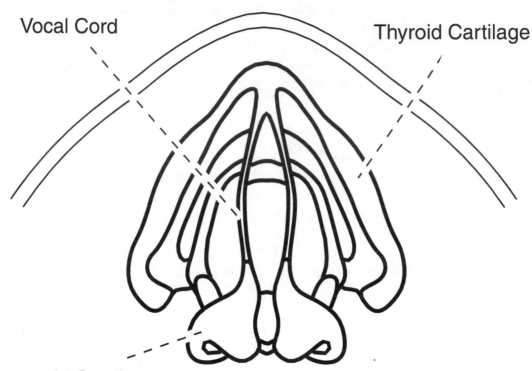

Arytenoid Cartilage

NOTE THAT THIS DIAGRAM IS NOT DRAWN TO SCALE. IN HIS BOOK, *TRADITION AND GIGLI*, E. HERBERT-CAESARI DESCRIBES THE SIZE OF THE VOCAL CORDS: "IN WOMEN, THE NORMAL LENGTH OF THE VOCAL CORDS IS HALF AN INCH, AND IN MEN, THREE QUARTERS OF AN INCH; EXCEPTIONALLY IN BOTH CASES, THEY MAY BE UP TO ONE INCH IN LENGTH (AS WERE CARUSO'S)."[3]

---

3   Excerpted with permission from Alma Caesari-Gramatke, from *Tradition and Gigli*, by E. Herbert-Caesari, Chapter III, "The Completely Natural Voice", p. 42, copyright by Alma and Rolf Gramatke, London NW6 7QS, 41 Mowbray Road.

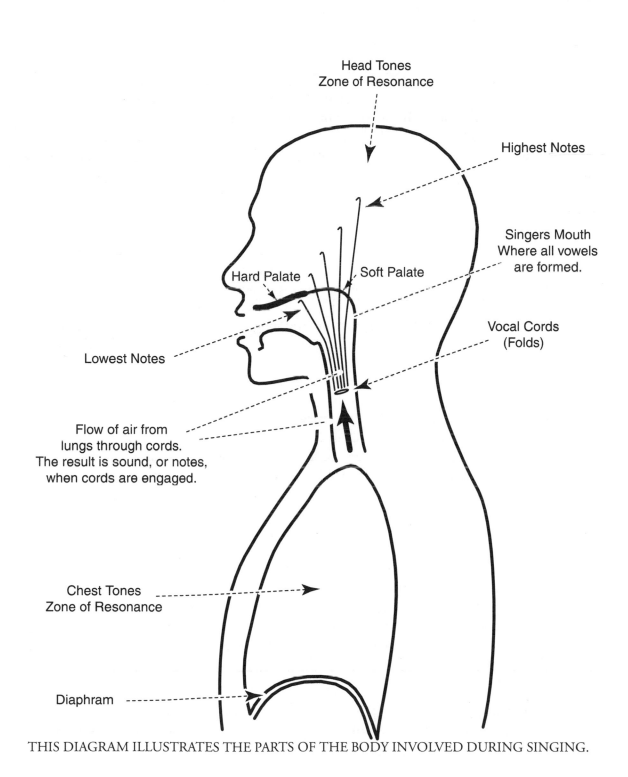

Head Tones
Zone of Resonance

Highest Notes

Singers Mouth
Where all vowels
are formed.

Hard Palate

Soft Palate

Vocal Cords
(Folds)

Lowest Notes

Flow of air from
lungs through cords.
The result is sound, or notes,
when cords are engaged.

Chest Tones
Zone of Resonance

Diaphram

THIS DIAGRAM ILLUSTRATES THE PARTS OF THE BODY INVOLVED DURING SINGING.

BREATHING

As I mentioned earlier, breathing is 80% of singing. Not too many people know that. But what is a note really? It is vibrating air! I give all my students the breathing exercise that you will find at the end of this chapter. It increases lung capacity tremendously. Once completed, you will never have to think about breathing again! One of the biggest problems singers have is in controlling their air. If you master this breathing exercise, you will be able to perform any song with ease.

RHYTHM

Rhythm is another vital part of music. Rhythm is the "heartbeat" of the song. Some people call the rhythm the "groove"—it's what you bob your head to, tap your feet to or dance to. If a band can't keep good time you won't be able to play together and you may not all end the song together. If the rhythm is not steady and solid, you will lose the audience. If the band and the singer can't agree on and keep the same rhythm, the song won't communicate to the audience because it won't hang together and give the audience something it can predict and relate to.

Listen to some songs and find the rhythm or groove of the song. It can be fast or slow—it doesn't matter. Find the groove and see if you can clap along with it. When you find the groove, everything will get in sync and it will feel effortless. If you still have trouble finding the groove in a song, try the rhythm exercises I've included on pages 25-28. These are the rhythm exercises that I give to my own students. If you are not having problems with rhythm, you should still do these exercises because they will help increase your rhythmic awareness as well as improve your sight reading.

Rhythm Exercises[4]

When doing these or any rhythmic drills, keep a fixed time base such as a metronome, click track, or drum machine. An important point to remember, however, is never play *to* the metronome—play *with* it! Use it as a guide to a particular tempo, then *duplicate* the tempo mentally and simply do what the metronome is doing. Too much dependence on an external fixed time base can produce "stiff" time (good tempo but no groove). So by doing what I suggest,

---

4   These rhythm exercises are adapted from *The Contemporary Keyboardist*, by John Novello (Warner Brothers Publications Inc., 15800 N.W. 48th Ave., Miami, Florida 33014 U.S.A., 1986) and used with permission.

you eventually won't need the metronome. You will have developed your own sense of accurate tempo plus still be able to groove.

Exercise 1

There are nine different ways to subdivide a beat, as illustrated in the diagram on the following page. But actually, there are really only four subdivisions: (1) Rhythm 1 has no subdivisions; (2) Rhythm 2 is division of a beat in half; (3) Rhythm 3 is division of a beat in thirds; and (4) Rhythm 4 is division of a beat in fourths. Rhythms 5 through 9 are basically permutations of Rhythm 4, so are still considered subdivisions of the beat in fourths. (A permutation is a change or alteration of a set of objects in a group, or, in this case, a set of notes.) In addition to subdivisions of a beat in fourths, there are subdivisions in groups of 5, 6, 7, 8, and so on.[5]

By either clapping or playing a single note on the piano, play each basic rhythm, as indicated in the diagram on the following page, until it is accurate, effortless, and in time. Use a metronome setting of about ♩ = 72 and count each rhythm out loud as indicated. Make sure you are relaxed before beginning this exercise.

When you have mastered the nine basic rhythms, do Exercise 2, which will improve your phrasing when singing.

---

5   See John Novello's *Contemporary Keyboardist Video Series*, Tape #2, "Rhythm, Improvisation, and the Blues," for more information on the nine basic rhythms (Warner Brothers Publications Inc., 15800 N.W. 48th Ave., Miami, Florida 33014 U.S.A., 1986).

1. No subdivision of beat

2. Subdivision of beat in 2

3. Subdivision of beat in 3

4. Subdivision of beat in 4

5. Subdivision of beat in 4

6. Subdivision of beat in 4

7. Subdivision of beat in 4

8. Subdivision of beat in 4

9. Subdivision of beat in 4

THE NINE BASIC RHYTHMS

Exercise 2

Practice transitioning at random from one basic rhythm to another without losing the tempo or rhythm. The most difficult transition is going from a division of three (rhythm 3) to a division of 2 or 4 (for example, 𝅘𝅥𝅮𝅘𝅥𝅮𝅘𝅥𝅮 to 𝅘𝅥𝅮𝅘𝅥𝅮).

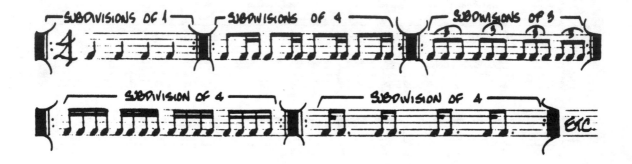

It helps to recognize in advance what subdivision you're transitioning to. Knowing if it's a subdivision in 1, 2, 3, or 4 and how to count it is the key to learning any rhythm. Once learned, however, you'll simply hear subdivisions and consequently be able to sing them without counting.

For a more detailed explanation of rhythm, see *The Contemporary Keyboardist*, by John Novello, Chapter 4, pp. 25-27.

WHAT KEY SHOULD I SING IN?

Many singers aren't aware that finding the right key for their voice is a very important part of being able to really get into a song and sing it well. If a song is in the right key, then you can really let go and have fun with it.

Just because you can't sing along with your favorite singer and hit all the notes doesn't mean you're not a good singer. The song may not be in the right key for your voice. No professional singer would ever consider singing a song that was in the wrong key for his or her voice. So why would you do something a professional wouldn't do?

On some occasions a producer will demand that a vocalist sing a song in a key that is not right for him or her because that *song* sounds better in a certain key. Remember that if you agree to do that, you may have difficulty singing the song and might not give your best performance. This, of course, will not be the best PR (public relations) for you, will it? The producer's goal, in that case, is a little off base, because the whole idea is, or should be, to feature the vocalist singing a really great song!

The only exception would be if you were doing a song demo for a songwriter and the song is being recorded for a particular artist. In that case the writer should find a singer who can sing the song in the key the writer wants the song to be recorded in.

I always use a standard rule of thumb for finding the right key for my songs. While I sing the song, I have the keyboardist (in my case it's my husband) play the song in the original key. Then he plays the song a little higher than the original key. Next he plays it a little lower than the original key. By having me sing through the song in three or four different keys, I'm able to find where it's most comfortable and where the "fat" (strongest part) of my voice is. I have a very wide range and I like to use the upper part of my voice as well as the very lowest part. So the correct key is usually where I have some head room on top as well as some room on the bottom to improvise with.

Some singers have asked me if they should sing all songs in the same key. Not necessarily. Different songs sound best in different keys that still work with your vocal range. True, you may sing some types of songs in the same key, like blues. I sing most blues and blues-based songs in the key of C. The more experience you get as a vocalist, the more easily you'll know when the key is correct or not.

SINGING IN TUNE

Being able to sing in tune is VITAL to becoming a good singer in any style of music. Singing out of tune is one of the first ways to get yourself kicked out of a band or to lose a studio gig. If you have problems singing in tune, it *must* be handled. If you don't know if you sing out of tune, you'd better find out fast. As mentioned in Chapter 2, a good vocal coach will able to help you in this area. You should be given some ear training exercises that first test your skill in singing in tune, and others that train you to develop perfect relative pitch.[6]

---

6   **Perfect relative pitch for a singer.** Given a note, this is the ability to identify and sing any other note. This is done by being able to hold a key center (the note that is your reference point) and identify intervals.

Occasionally I'll hear a singer say, "Well if I sing out of tune, it can be fixed in the studio with some of the special gear they use on your voice to make it sound better." You'd better think again, because record companies and producers don't want to work with a singer who can't sing in tune. It wastes money and time. Chances are if you sing out of tune you won't make it past the producer to even get into the studio. And most often you'll have to do a live performance for record executives. If you sing out of tune when you audition for them, you run a big risk of blowing the deal. Every time I'm asked to recommend a singer to a producer or manager or record company, the very first question is, "Can they sing in tune?"

TONE DEAFNESS

Many times during a conversation with someone who loved to sing at some earlier time, I have found that they were steered away from singing merely because they were told that they were "tone deaf." Once you agree with this, then guess what? You are!

What is "tone deafness"? Actually, there is no such thing as tone deafness. When a person is supposedly tone deaf, it's simply an inability to duplicate a tone or sound. Technically, it's when the mind doesn't make a copy of (duplicate) the sound the individual is hearing. It's no different than when you put a document into a copy machine, press the "print" button but the copy comes out blank. Someone in this situation is the exact opposite of someone with a "good ear."

However, tone deafness is a very simple problem to handle if the correct exercises and drills are done. I use several exercises, depending on the degree of the individual's inability to duplicate sounds. Sometimes there are people who can't hear the difference between two notes, one of them high and the other low. This would be the most extreme case, but it can be handled. I've successfully trained a person who was unable to sing even a single note in tune or recognize a high note from a low one. After I worked with her for six months on various exercises, she became able to work regularly as a vocalist and has no problems staying in tune!

Because of experiences such as the above, I keep coming back to the same statement: if you have a good vocal teacher or coach, they will be able to help you handle this problem... and *without* hurting your feelings!

If you think you have a problem with being able to hear the notes and duplicate them correctly, plan on correcting these problems before you go out on an audition and before you perform. The ear training exercises at the end of this chapter will help you with any difficulties you may have hearing and singing notes accurately. Note that the exercises for handling tone deafness are specialized exercises that I've developed and are best done with someone who is trained in my method.

EAR TRAINING[7]

What is ear training and why is it so important? What is the ear's relationship to the eye and the voice, and what is the relationship of all three (ears, eyes, voice) to your mind and to you?

Well, actually, the ear and the eye are your *antennae* and are hooked up to your brain—switchboard—through which you, the "operator," call the shots according to the information received. In other words, the eye looks, that you may see, and the ear listens, that you may hear, so that you, the operator, may control your voice.

Now although both senses—eye and ear—are important, which is more important to you, the singer? Yes, that's right—the *ear*!

The ear is the judge! Educate the ear, and problems playing *your* instrument—your voice—as well as problems with technique, improvisation, phrasing, style duplication, intonation, etc.—whatever it may be—simply fall by the wayside.

The ear is both receptive and directive. In other words, it is receptive in that it receives sound images from within (the creative faculties of the imagination) as well as actual sounds from instruments outside. And the ear is directive in that with this information, it can direct the voice. So educate your ear and you'll be happening!

Now in reality, it's not actually the *ear* we're training, it's *you*—you the individual, the spirit, the intelligence who's in charge. But, as explained above, the ear is the conduit, or receiver, for most of this information—that's why we use the term "ear training."

The goal of ear training is to enable you to simultaneously identify, differentiate, and process certain levels of musical information primarily sensed through the ear—melody, harmony, rhythm and dynamics, to name a few. This results in the composite skills and actions of performing.

---

7   The following discussion of ear training is adapted with permission from *The Contemporary Keyboardist*, by John Novello (Warner Brothers Publications Inc., 15800 N.W. 48th Ave., Miami, Florida 33014 U.S.A., 1986).

The ability to hear these levels of musical information simultaneously is a basic prerequisite for effortless performances and the mark of a natural and confident musician—and singers *are* musicians! The ear training exercises at the end of the chapter are designed to zero in on these levels and improve your musical sensitivity. So the drills should not be regarded as an end in themselves, but as a means to attain this sensitivity.

I hope this puts into perspective the importance of the ear—the judge!

At the end of this chapter are some excellent ear training exercises.[8] Make sure you understand the following definitions before you begin the exercises:

Perfect Pitch or **Absolute Pitch.** The ability to determine a note from its frequency or rate of vibration alone, along with the ability to sing or name a note asked for.

Perfect Relative Pitch for a Singer. Given a note, the ability to identify and sing any other note. This is done by being able to hold a key center and identify intervals. A key center is the note that is your reference point.

RECORD COPYING

What's a record copy? That's when you copy a record, CD or cassette by singing the song like the artist sings it. Contrary to what some people might say, it's not bad for you to do this, and you won't come out sounding like the artist on the record if you do this exercise correctly.

What is the purpose of doing record copies? To have you learn from established artists things like phrasing, emoting, rhythm, vocal lines, ad libs and more. When you duplicate their style it helps you to create your own. What better way to learn something than from someone whose vocal abilities you admire and respect? In every field of the arts—acting, painting, dancing, writing and music—artists do copies of famous artists they love and respect. It's a way of learning. Michael Jackson said he watched a lot of Fred Astaire movies. And if you watch an old Fred Astaire movie, you'll see how his dance moves inspired a lot of Michael's moves. Watch The Artist Formerly Known as Prince and compare his moves to James Brown.

---

8   The ear training exercises at the end of this chapter are a from *The Contemporary Keyboardist*, by John Novello (Warner Brothers Publications Inc., 15800 N.W. 48th Ave., Miami, Florida 33014 U.S.A., 1986) and used with permission.

By the way, one of the main reasons you don't have to worry about sounding like the singer you copy is because you have *your* vocal cords and the singer you copy has his or her own. No two sets are ever the same. Additionally, no one can ever copy exactly what another artist does because the person copying the artist is a unique individual, and so is the original artist. The person doing the copying can't ever be the original artist—he can only be himself.

Thus, record copying is one of the most important and vital steps you can take in developing your own style. The whole idea is to duplicate as closely as possible what the original artist did, learn something in the process, and then *make it your own.* Making a song your own is a big responsibility and hard work. Don't get discouraged if you find it difficult at first—it gets easier the more you do it.

After you have done copies from about 50 or 100 different artists and have learned a little from each one and have made each one your own—and then, after you've done a few hundred gigs and have studied your fundamentals—you'll be on your way to developing your own style. This process takes as long as it takes! So be concerned with improving your ability, not with how long it's taking. By the way, studying your singing and music fundamentals will make the record copying process easier.

IMPROVISING

Improvising is something every singer of contemporary styles of music needs to know how to do. This is when the singer changes or modifies the melody of the song while staying within the confines of the chords and key of the song. If you don't improvise in a song, then the song can become very boring and dull. Improvising is also called "riffing." If you go "outside" the chords (sing notes that are not contained in the chord progression or key) while improvising, you may cause tension and seem to clash—unless, of course, it's a style of singing where that is expected. (This is often done in certain types of jazz and avant-garde.) Just make sure that if you're singing "outside," you're doing it intentionally and not by accident!

When you are really creating a lot of emotion during a song, it's easy to improvise. A good teacher should be able to help you learn how to improvise. Another way you can learn to do this is by doing your record copies. Almost every singer you listen to will do some kind of improvising. If you're doing a record copy you should learn all the improvised lines as closely as possible. And sometimes you can "borrow" a line and put it into a different song, because you've made it your own. Most people will think it's yours anyway, because you have *made* it yours. You now "own" it.

Eventually, when you've done enough record copies of various artists, you will start to feel confident about your ad-libbing and begin to see your own style develop. This again is your postulates at work. When you practice, don't be afraid to take chances and play around with the melody and see how many ways you can sing it and still stay in the right key. Sometimes you may sing a note that's really off, but don't worry about it. That's why you practice—so you can see if certain notes work or not.

One good thing to do when you're improvising is to record yourself. This way, you don't have to try to listen to yourself at the same time you're singing. Listening to yourself while trying to improvise will have a really bad effect on your performance. To be able to improvise freely, you have to be able to create freely without any thoughts or considerations about how good or bad something sounds. So it's always better to record everything you sing and play it back and see if you want to keep it or not. If you want to keep it, then you have a recording of it for reference.

DUPLICATION SKILLS

Good duplication skills consist of the ability to hear a note or series of notes and sing exactly what you hear. A good singer has this ability. If you have good duplication skills, it's not unusual to have someone tell you that you have a "good ear." People who "play by ear" (and don't read music) usually have good duplication skills: they rely on their ear to duplicate what they hear. Of course, in the long run, it is better to be fully trained and then still "sing by ear." But then, oh, what an ear, as it's a trained ear with much more headroom and diversity!

READING MUSIC—IS IT A MUST?

It's always an advantage to know how to read music. However, there are many singers who have become very successful who don't even know where middle C is on a piano. If you want to become a session singer and do jingles (commercials), then it's a very good idea to know how to read music and read well. But once again, there are lots of singers who don't read music, yet still make good livings as session singers. Let me put it this way—you'll get a lot more jobs if you know how to read music than if you don't.

One more thing about reading: being able to do it will give you more of an advantage when you're working with trained musicians, producers, arrangers and songwriters. Among male musicians, especially trained musicians, there is a stigma that is sometimes attached to female singers in the industry. They're known as "chick singers"—an endearing little term that sticks with them until they prove they can "hang" with the other musicians musically, hold their own and not be pushed around. Knowing how to read music helps a singer to avoid being stuck with that negative label. Handling the "chick singer" vibe is discussed further in chapter 9, "The Business Side of the Business."

PRACTICE DISCIPLINES[9]

Adequate practice is vital to your being able to improve your singing ability and achieve your goals. I have observed that the students who progress the fastest and the furthest are those who understand how to practice. This makes practice one of the most basic and important skills of a singer—or any musician. Therefore, I make it standard procedure to thoroughly orient a student to the "ideal scene" of practicing in order that both the student and I reap the best results. Excuses such as "I didn't practice this week because—" are simply not acceptable.

Before we look at a standard operating procedure for practicing, here are a few terms we need to define:

1. **Pre-practice,** the period right before actually practicing where you set the goals for the session.

2. **Practice,** the actual "doingness" where you are trying to achieve a certain ability through repetition, as well as the "think" involved in evaluation, attention to detail, reevaluation, and comparison to the ideal scene. Practice is the time when you should have your attention on improving your skill and what you are doing—*not* while performing! This practice time should also include ear training and rhythm exercises. **Please note:** The maximum time you should devote to doing scales, etc., is two hours.

3. **Post-practice,** the time for comparison of what you have just done in the practice session with what you intended to do, so as to determine what the next session's content should be.

4. **Singing** is simply singing! It is using whatever technical expertise you have to express yourself to the audience. If there is any kind of "think" going on, then to that degree you are not singing.

5. **Objective Self Criticism,** becoming self-sufficient at being your own critic. This ability allows the student to eventually dispense with his or her teacher, if desired, and free himself or herself as an artist!

---

9   "Practice Disciplines" is excerpted from the book *The Contemporary Keyboardist,* by John Novello (Warner Brothers Publications Inc., 15800 N.W. 48th Ave., Miami, Florida 33014 U.S.A., 1986) and used with permission.

Organizing Practice Sessions

After making sure you understand the above definitions, you should read and carry out the following steps for organizing practice sessions:

1. Form an honest conviction toward achieving your goal or goals—for example, to be a great R&B singer.

2. Decide to set aside a minimum amount of time each day for practice. Start low and gradually increase the amount of time per day.

3. Each day, graph your *honestly done practice hours* in order to keep an accurate record. This is important because you'll want to know if your statistics are rising, staying consistent, or falling. If they're falling, you'll need to quickly reorganize your time to increase your practice! The illustrations on the next pages show examples of graphs for practice time.

4. Create your day the night before. This simply means to plan a time schedule of your whole day and include, of course, *your practice time.*

Practice Hours - Daily

Total Hrs For The Week ___17___

IF YOU HAVE A GRAPH THAT LOOKS LIKE THIS BY THE END OF THE WEEK, THEN YOU HAVE DONE WELL.

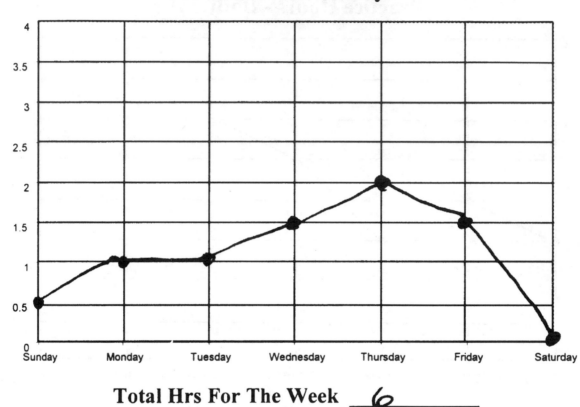

Practice Hours - Daily

Total Hrs For The Week _6_

IF, ON THE OTHER HAND, THE FOLLOWING WEEK YOUR GRAPH LOOKS LIKE THIS, IT'S NOT A GOOD SIGN—UNLESS YOU HAD A GIG IN WHICH YOU WERE SINGING. YOU NEED TO REEVALUATE YOUR DAY AND FIGURE OUT WHAT WENT WRONG SO YOU CAN FIX IT. BASED ON THE "STUDENT PROGRESS EVALUATION" AT THE END OF THIS SECTION, THIS IS JUST BELOW AVERAGE.

At the back of the book I've provided you with several blank graphs you can pull out, copy and use to keep track of your own practice hours.

Sample Practice Schedules

If you have a straight job, your schedule might look like this:

7:30 AM-	8:30 AM	Up, shower, breakfast
8:30 AM-	9:00 AM	Travel to work
9:00 AM-	5:00 PM	Job
5:00 PM-	5:30 PM	Travel home
5:30 PM-	7:00 PM	Dinner
7:00 PM-	8:00 PM	Relax
8:00 PM-	8:15 PM	Pre-practice reflection
8:15 PM-	9:30 PM	Practice
9:30 PM-	9:45 PM	Post-practice reflection
9:45 PM-	11:00 PM	Leisure
	11:00 PM	Bed

However, if you're a full-time singer, your schedule might look like this:

10:00 AM-	11:00 AM	Up, shower, breakfast
11:00 AM-	11:15 AM	Pre-practice reflection
11:15 AM-	1:15 PM	Practice
1:15 PM-	1:30 PM	Post-practice reflection
1:30 PM-	2:00 PM	Lunch
2:00 PM-	3:00 PM	Promote career
3:00 PM-	6:00 PM	Rehearsal for gig
6:00 PM-	7:00 PM	Dinner
7:00 PM-	8:00 PM	Travel to gig and set up
8:00 PM-	1:00 AM	Night gig
	1:00 AM	Home and bed

Following such a schedule each day starts you on the road to being in control over your life, thus increasing your chances for success. When you hold yourself to a schedule, you are a lot less subject to the random occurrences and distractions that life brings and that can eat up your time—and your chances for a career! If you stick to this schedule, eventually you'll find yourself creating weeks at a time in advance, and more!

Practice Procedure

The four steps for organizing practice sessions (page 37) allow you to organize and create time so you can get on with the business of practicing. What follows, therefore, is a standard procedure for the actual practice session.

1. If possible, leave your problems outside the practice room. If that is not possible, then it's probably better that you handle whatever it is your attention is on and *then* practice. Otherwise the practice session might be very glib (superficial, insincere)—in other words, you might not really get anything from it, but may just be going through the motions.

2. Shift your attention to the goals you have created for the session, and when you feel ready to start, then say out loud:

3. "START!" I have found that most students never *really* start the practice session. Simply randomly singing a few songs or parts of songs is not practicing. Therefore, giving yourself a verbal start makes the session a little more real and important.

4. Organize your allotted time by practicing the most difficult things first, when you're fresh, and the easiest things last. Also make sure you cover everything you planned—especially if you have a limited amount of time. However, if you just can't cover everything, make a note of where you left off and begin there at your next practice session.

5. Be aware of your emotions, for they can get in the way. Boredom, anger, depression, grief, etc., can take the "attack" out of the session. If you become aware of negative emotions, get up and take a five-minute break and then resume. Enthusiasm is the emotion necessary for successful practice sessions. If you take your time and practice things gradiently—that is, progress gradually—you won't stir up negative emotions.

6. When you've either completed your targets or your allotted time, end the practice part of the session and give yourself a "well done" (mentally or out loud). But there's still one more very important step—

7. Now SING! Sing anything! It may or may not be related to your lesson, but just sing. Always sing after you practice because that's what you're practicing for—remember? Now, singing by itself has no "think" associated with it—no evaluation or consideration of how you're doing. That part of the session is over. Just imagine you're singing for an audience and simply sing! Don't stop, even if there are mistakes. Singing is the real thing and a professional performance means you're in control. If you ever get a chance to ask a great artist what's going on while he or she is performing, you'll find that they usually can't explain it. That's because there's *nothing* going on. If the artist is prepared—meaning he or she's done her homework—then the *only* thing going on is "singing."

If applied honestly, this practice procedure will pave the way for you to advance rapidly and realize your potentials in a relatively short time. It is not true that it has to take eight to ten hours per day and twenty years to become a real professional. With good guidance, diligence, and organized practice, you can become very good in a relatively short time.

Student Progress Evaluation

Use this Student Progress Evaluation to evaluate your progress toward attaining your goal to improve your ability as a vocalist. This practice time should also include ear training and rhythm exercises. **Please note:** The maximum time you should devote to doing scales, etc., is two hours.

> **Superlative:** Lessons 3 to 5 times per week, shows up on time for every lesson, completes all lesson assignments, practices 21 hours per week or more, progressing at an incredible rate, pays all tuition promptly.

> **Above Average:** Lessons 2 to 3 times per week, shows up for every lesson, completes all lesson assignments, practices 14 or more hours per week, progressing at a good rate, pays all tuition promptly.

> **Average:** One lesson per week, shows up for most of lessons and occasionally late, completes most lesson assignments, practices 7 or more hours per week, progressing at an average rate, pays tuition but has to be reminded occasionally.

> **Subaverage:** Misses lessons frequently for all kinds of reasons, has trouble completing lesson assignments, practices only about 3 hours a week if that, progressing but very slowly, needs constant reminding to pay tuition.

> **Unsatisfactory:** Misses many lessons and constantly shows up late, never completes lesson assignments, rarely practices, behind in tuition, not progressing at all, bad checks, etc.

EXERCISES

1. Practice postulating notes.

2. Write down on a sheet of paper a list of times you communicated to someone through a song, through the way you were dressed or through some other artistic means.

3. Make a list of times when an artist communicated to you through a song, a painting, a photograph, etc.

4. Think of some examples of when you observed an artist putting too much attention on technical expertise. What effect did it have on you?

5. Make a list of times you focused on technical expertise and how it affected your ability to communicate each time.

6. Using a good medical chart, locate the parts of the vocal apparatus. Find the vocal cords, larynx, pharynx, diaphragm, and lungs. For the best reference guide to the parts of the voice, I recommend that you order the books mentioned earlier in this chapter.

7. Start the breathing exercise.

8. Start the rhythm exercises.

9. Check your songs to make certain they are in the right key for your voice.

10. Start the ear training exercises.

11. Find a song you like and do lots of record copies.

12. Experiment around with improvising a song you know very well. After you're comfortable, find a new one to start on.

13. Take a look at how reading music is going to help you in your career. If you decide you want to improve that ability, I recommend the *Contemporary Keyboardist Video Series*, Tape I, "The Basics."

14. Apply the steps in the section above, "Organizing Practice Sessions," to your next practice session.

THE BREATHING EXERCISE

Introduction

This excellent breathing exercise, developed by E. Herbert-Caesari,[10] will increase your lung capacity tremendously and give you greater breath control in your singing. It will take you about twelve weeks, plus or minus, to complete. Note that if you are a current swimmer or play a wind instrument, you may not need to do this exercise, because your lung capacity may already be at its full potential. However, if you wish to carry out the exercise anyway, you may begin at ten seconds rather than four seconds.

Make sure no one will interrupt you during your breathing exercise each day. If you are $2\frac{1}{2}$ minutes into the exercise and stop, you will have to begin again at the beginning. You can't pick up where you left off, but must do the entire exercise cycle continuously for five minutes.

Special care should be taken not to cram the lungs full of air by inhaling too fast. If you inhale too much air you will have more air in your lungs than you can exhale in the allotted number of seconds. During the exercise, breathe through your nose, not your mouth. Use a clock or watch with a second hand, or a digital clock, to count the seconds in this exercise. It is easy to count too fast or slow, and if you do, you won't get the full benefit of the exercise.

One final note: This is a very boring exercise and you will have a tendency to not want to do it! Keep in mind that, as I mentioned before, singing is 80% breath control. Master this exercise and you'll be 80% there! Make up some kind of schedule or plan. To get you started, I suggest you do Section A (First Two Weeks) for five minutes before you get out of bed in the morning; for five minutes sometime during the day; and the last cycle five minutes before you go to sleep at bedtime.

Procedure

A. First Two Weeks

1. Lie down.

---

10   Grateful acknowledgment is made to Alma Caesari-Gramatke for permission to adopt portions of the breathing exercise from *The Science and Sensations of Vocal Tone* (J.M. Dent. Ltd., London, 1977), by E. Herbert-Caesari, Addenda, page 177 (out of print at date of publication of this book).

2. Close or plug up one of your nostrils. If it is easier to breathe out of one side of your nose than the other, leave that side open. You do not have to switch nostrils during the course of the entire exercise.

3. Inhale for a count of 4 seconds.

4. Hold for a count of 4 seconds.

5. Exhale for a count of 4 seconds.

6. Then immediately inhale again for 4 seconds, hold for 4 and out for 4 as in steps 3-5.

7. Repeat this breathing exercise cycle (4-4-4) for 5 minutes with no interruption.

For best results, this exercise should be done three times a day, every day, for a period of two weeks.

B. Third Week

Now increase the time to 6 seconds, and do the exercise *sitting up.*

Important: You should *never* increase to the next interval of seconds if you have not mastered the interval you are working on. For example, if you are working on 4 seconds and are having problems with it, DO NOT increase to 6 seconds. It will be impossible to do. Continue with 4 seconds until you master it.

1. Inhale for a count of 6 seconds.

2. Hold for a count of 6 seconds.

3. Exhale for a count of 6 seconds.

4. Repeat this breathing exercise cycle (6-6-6) for 5 minutes with no interruption.

Perform the exercise three times daily for 5 minutes each time, for one week.

C. Fourth Week

Now increase the time to 8 seconds, and do the exercise *standing.*

1. Inhale for a count of 8 seconds.

2. Hold for a count of 8 seconds.

3. Exhale for a count of 8 seconds.

4. Repeat this breathing exercise cycle (8-8-8) for 5 minutes with no interruption.

Perform the exercise three times daily for 5 minutes each time, for one week.

D. Subsequent Weeks

Provided you have no problems with 8 seconds, increase to 10 seconds. The 10-second exercise and all the following ones should also be performed standing.

Each week you will increase by 2 seconds until you reach 20 seconds inhaling, 20 seconds holding, and 20 seconds exhaling.

EAR TRAINING EXERCISES

Exercise 1 - Perfect Relative Pitch

Objective: Given any note—in this case C—to be able to identify any of the other eleven notes (twelve if you include C).

Procedure:

1. Create an aural mental image of C by playing it on the piano until you can sing it, as well as "hear" it in your mind. Playing a standard chord progression such as I - IV - V - IV - I will definitely help define the key center if you're having problems. (For example, playing I - IV - V - IV - I in the key of C means playing chords C major to F major to G major to F major to C major.)

2. Either by closing your eyes or turning your back to the piano, hit any note, preferably in your vocal range for now, with the eraser end of a long pencil. By comparing the just-struck note with the one that's hopefully still in your head, you should eventually be able to identify the interval and thus the note. Your answer should pretty much occur within two seconds. We're trying to develop the intuitive response. Too long a time and too much "think" is no good, even if you get the note right. If you don't know, make a guess. You might be surprised how many you'll get right this way. Intuition, "gut feeling," "going for it"—whatever you call it—sometimes seems elusive, but is *always* very powerful, once developed!

This should be done for a few minutes every day until you can do it consistently. It takes as long as it takes. After all, you're only trying to develop perfect relative pitch—give yourself a break! Six months to a year to develop this ability is not uncommon.

Exercise 2 - Reverse Relative Pitch

Objective: Given a note—in this case C—to be able to sing any other note.

Procedure:

1. As in Exercise 1, get C in your mind.

2. Point to any note within your vocal range and sing it.

3. Check to see if you're right by sounding the note.

4. Repeat Steps 1 through 3.

The difference between this exercise and Exercise 1 is that in the first exercise, you are trying to identify a sound after hearing it, while in Exercise 2 you are asked to sing a sound on command. Since these abilities, along with creativity, are what singing is all about, you'll find these exercises very helpful.

Exercise 3 - Half Step Whole Step

Objective: Given any note, to be able to sing a half step up or down, and a whole step up or down. Although this exercise can be done with any interval, half steps and whole steps are the most beneficial. After you have mastered half steps and whole steps, try other intervals such as thirds, fourths, fifths, etc.

Procedure:

1. Play note (staccato).

2. Sing desired note (staccato) a half or whole step up or down.

CHAPTER 4

SINGING FOR AN AUDIENCE: PERFORMANCE BASICS

STAGE PRESENCE - WHAT IS IT?

Stage presence is having the ability to project a sense of ease and poise or self-assurance, before an audience, as defined in *The Random House Dictionary*.

Let's take a look at exactly what that means. If you do any of the following things while you're performing, your stage presence will suffer. And it will suffer to the degree your attention is directed to them.

1. Wondering what the audience is thinking.

2. Wondering if the audience likes you.

3. Worried if your hair or other parts of your costume look good.

4. Hoping you don't forget the words.

5. Worried about the bright lights being in your eyes.

6. Thinking about the fight you had with your boyfriend or girlfriend.

7. Disliking the audience.

8. Thinking the audience is stupid.

9. Listening to yourself instead of the band or track (musical accompaniment) you're singing to.

10. Bored with the songs you're singing.

11. Don't like the songs you're singing.

12. Nervous about being onstage and/or in front of a group of people.

13. Thinking you're too good for the audience you're singing for.

14. Worried about what to do with your body.

I could go on and on with things that singers often *think* and do while onstage. The bottom line is that A SINGER ISN'T SUPPOSED TO DO ANYTHING ELSE ONSTAGE BUT SING. That's your *job*—to sing. If you do anything else but SING you are not doing your job to the best of your ability. One little known but very important fact is that EVERYTHING YOU THINK AND FEEL AND CREATE DURING YOUR PERFORMANCE IS FELT BY YOUR AUDIENCE. That's right! If you don't like your audience, they will know it! If you're afraid of the audience, they will feel that, too. Why is that? Certainly in large part, it's because singing is an art and art is a communication. Remember the section about communication in Chapter 3? (If you need to review that section, now would be a good time to do so.)

How many times have you been to a concert or heard a band at a local night spot, and the band played and the singer sang, but you and the rest of the audience paid no attention to them? You actually felt the band was annoying you and interrupting your conversation. That's the perfect example of a singer and a band that didn't have good command of the audience and very little stage presence. The band probably had one or more symptoms from the above list.

On the other hand, if you look at an accomplished, confident performer, you'll notice one thing about them—they don't look like they're worried about forgetting words or whether you like them or not. The Artist Formerly Known as Prince is a perfect example of someone who has incredible stage presence. Others who have it are Madonna, Stevie Wonder, Clint Black, Barbra Streisand, Luciano Pavarotti, Maria Callas and Kathleen Battle. Do you think Stevie wonders if people don't like him because he's visually impaired? Whitney Houston isn't concerned about a dance routine or her lack of participation in it while she sings. Luther Vandross isn't concerned about his weight when he sings. I hope you get the point. They focus on singing and performing for the audience. The other things may come up, of course, but they don't bring that baggage on stage.

So take a look at what your responsibility is as an artist. Think about what your audience would get from you if you had everything in the above list going on in your communication!

But, you say, "How do I get rid of my stage fright, stop having all those thoughts about myself, and achieve good stage presence?" Let's say you sing great in front of a mirror or in the shower, but never in front of a group of people. Or maybe you're afraid to get up in front of a *big* group of people and sing. It doesn't matter if the group is small or large, stage fright is stage fright. Having a lot of random thoughts and worries about things that have nothing to do with communicating your song, or performing critiques of yourself while performing onstage, result in very little or no stage presence.

Many of my students have taken my four-week Stage Presence workshop. It's a videotaped class that has produced some wonderful results. In that class I show my students videos of some of my favorite performers at their live concerts. That way they get a real firsthand look at what the singers do while they're singing. I recommend you do this as well—get some videos of your favorite performers' live shows and check them out for yourself. See if you can figure out what they are thinking about when they sing. If you're fortunate enough to be able to go to a concert and see a singer live, do the same exercise. If the singer you go to see is really burning, you'll actually forget about the exercise and really get into the performance. But if his or her stage presence is lacking, your mind will start to wander and you'll begin talking to your friends or doing something else.

I know many of you reading this book don't live in the Los Angeles area and can't attend one of my workshops. If you live in a town where there isn't anyone who teaches a good performance workshop, don't worry—all is not lost! I have provided some exercises in the following sections that will help you over the rough periods and assist you in developing polished stage presence.

HOW TO HANDLE STAGE FRIGHT

Two factors that contribute to stage fright are not really knowing your material, and having uncertainty about your vocal ability. If you don't know your material, then you should keep practicing until you know the songs really well. If you're worried about your vocal ability, then it's time to take voice lessons to improve your voice. If you were a performer when you were a kid and stopped for a while, you may experience some stage fright getting back onstage again. However, that feeling can be overcome.

Drills for Stage Fright

I've come across various drills that you can do that will help to diminish or eliminate your stage fright.

1. Find an empty theater or auditorium and ask for permission to use it. Go up on the stage and just get used to being on the stage. Walk around until you start to feel comfortable onstage. Look around the stage, notice the things that are in the ceiling, behind the curtain and all around the stage. I know this might feel a little silly, but it's OK and it will help you start to feel comfortable being on a stage. Touch some of the things that make up the stage like the floor and curtains, microphone stand—whatever is onstage. In other words, make the stage *your* stage. By the way, if people have their equipment onstage, *always* make sure you ask permission before you go onstage. Musicians and singers are *very* touchy when it comes to their equipment for a variety of reasons, all of them completely valid. Maybe you

have a friend who will allow you to go on the stage before the audience comes into the room.

2. The next step to this exercise is to visualize, while onstage, that an audience is there watching you. You can make the audience any size you want. Keep in mind that since you visualized them, you can make them disappear anytime you want! So make them disappear. Keep doing this over and over again until you start to feel comfortable having an audience out there watching you. The more you do this little exercise, the more comfortable you will feel onstage. Soon you will be ready to confront a real audience.

3. There are a lot of karaoke rooms that have an open mic night for anyone who wants to get up and sing. If you'd like to start with a small audience, find a Karaoke room where there aren't a lot of people. Sign up to sing, but pick out a song you know very well, or bring your own Karaoke track. Ask the K.J. (Karaoke Jockey) if you can use your track. As long as it's in the same format as the Karaoke machine being used, there shouldn't be a problem. Most often the lyrics are played along with the Karaoke track, so if you find a song you don't know all the words to, they will be there right in front of you.

4. You can also get over stage fright by just singing onstage over and over again. That's how I overcame my stage fright. The first time is always the most difficult, but the first time only happens once. One of the reasons I developed my performance workshop was to help people get through the horrible "first time jitters." It's no fun at all and sometimes can be so bad you can make yourself sick.

The whole idea is that the more you sing before audiences, the more comfortable you'll become. Eventually you will lose your stage fright. Try some of the things I've suggested and see what happens. What have you got to lose but your stage fright?

PRE-PERFORMANCE NERVOUSNESS

Believe it or not, I've heard singers say they like the feeling of being nervous onstage. You may even hear a teacher say it's OK to feel nervous. The "nervousness" they are referring to is the excitement and rush you get when you're about to perform—when you feel ready and you know you're going to deliver a dynamite performance. So this is quite a different feeling from being nervous and *unsure about your ability to perform!* Singers can experience this pre-performance nervousness and still be perfectly comfortable and at ease onstage.

STAGE MANNERS

What are stage manners? Well, you know what table manners are, don't you? Table manners consist of acceptable behavior for the table. Well, you might not have known that there is acceptable behavior for the stage as well. Good stage manners are essential to having polished stage presence.

Remember the earlier list of things you shouldn't be doing when you're onstage to sing and entertain an audience? Number 13, "Think you're too good for the audience," is not good stage manners. Fidgeting, turning your back on the audience (unless it's part of your act), not acknowledging the audience's applause, not knowing what to do with yourself at any time while you're onstage—all these things are unacceptable behavior onstage. How many times have you seen a performer make a mistake onstage and tell you they made a mistake and apologize? I'll bet you felt sorry for the singer. I know I have when I've witnessed this. All that does is pull the audience's attention onto the mistake and make them feel very uncomfortable.

A young lady was performing in a talent show and she forgot the words. She stopped singing and told the audience she sang the wrong verse. It was obvious she was upset with herself and she fumbled around with the mic and asked the sound guy to start it again. Her performance never recovered. What should she have done? She should have continued just as if nothing had happened, even if she was singing the wrong words. If she had been really into the song in the first place, she wouldn't have forgotten the words. Even if she did sing the wrong words, but was still really into the song, the audience wouldn't have even known or cared.

I spoke with her manager after the show and offered my assistance. The manager saw she needed work but was being too protective and wouldn't let me speak to her. It isn't hard to imagine that she never wanted to sing again after that, as it was such a horrid experience for her. The last time I spoke with that manager, he told me she wasn't singing any more. That entire incident could have been avoided if the singer had had the right information and was given proper training.

You should also practice coming onstage, as well as leaving, with poise and dignity or the manner that is appropriate to your act. If you have a comedy act, then your entrance would be different than that of an opera singer. Neither one, however, would walk onstage like he or she is walking to the bathroom. Get the idea?

It would not be good stage manners to not know how to handle or use your equipment (mic or instruments). Get familiar with your microphone, the mic stand, the mic cord if there is one, your music stand, and the layout of the stage itself.

Remember the exercise on stage fright in the above section, in which you go around and touch things on the stage? Well, now you know why it's important to do that—so you will become comfortable handling the tools necessary for you to do your job.

You should be willing to stand onstage and do nothing but be admired by the audience. Never, ever invalidate or ignore the audience's applause for you, even if you feel you did a lousy show. When the audience applauds you, it's their way of telling you they liked what you did. They're thanking you.

Most importantly, if an audience member comes up to you after your show and tells you how great you were, thank him or her. Never, never EVER make excuses for yourself or the band if a mistake was made during the show. If the audience member liked it, then let him leave with that good memory of you and your band. If you tell him, "Yeah, but I sang all the wrong words and the band made a mistake...." then it makes the audience member wrong for thinking it was good. YOU'VE JUST "DISRESPECTED" HIS OPINION AND INVALIDATED HIS VIEWPOINT. Keep your comments about all the wrong things you did to yourself and discuss it with your band members later when you're practicing.

If you want to know more about stage manners, read the book, *Art*, by L. Ron Hubbard. Chapter 15 of *Art* explains the fundamentals of stage manners and contains a drill you can use to improve your stage manners and stage presence.

DO ACTING LESSONS HELP?

Yes! Without a doubt, acting lessons will help you improve your performance skills as a singer and gain confidence onstage. Before I had my first acting class, I was afraid to be onstage unless I was singing a song, and I was afraid to talk to the audience. Acting lessons helped me achieve the ability to be comfortable onstage while doing nothing else and to speak freely and easily to an audience. They will also help you if you have no stage experience of any kind and are intimidated at the thought of getting onstage.

Gaining confidence onstage will improve your stage presence. I have been told on a number of occasions that I have great stage presence, and I can say with absolute certainty that I do! It's not arrogance or conceit to feel that way about an ability. On the contrary, the confidence itself reinforces and enhances my stage presence. It's okay to have confidence in yourself.

One of my students, a shy young man in his teens, took acting lessons. It was the best thing he could have done to improve his singing. He overcame his shyness and learned how to create and communicate emotion in his songs. He can create a different character for each song.

HOW TO MAKE A SONG REAL TO THE AUDIENCE

When you sing, you need to know how to create the place (environment) suggested in the song. You need to be able to communicate exactly where you were at that moment in time when you felt the emotions you're singing about. And you need to be able to do this whether you're singing to a live audience or into a mic in the studio. I'll give you an example of what I'm talking about.

Let's say the lyrics of a song you're singing go something like this:

"FEEL LIKE I CAN FLY, IS IT JUST BECAUSE YOU'RE TOUCHING ME?"

Obviously whoever is singing this line feels really good because somebody is touching them. In preparing to sing the song, here are some questions the singer should know the answers to:

1. If you feel like you can fly, are you inside or outside?

2. If you're outside, are you at the beach, on a mountaintop, or at the Grand Canyon?

3. Is it raining, cloudy, sunny with billowy clouds, hot, cold, windy? What's the weather like?

4. Who's touching you? A lover, parent, other relative? What does the person look like? Is it the man or woman of your dreams? What color hair?

5. Where did this person touch you? On the hand?

6. How did this person touch you? By accident? Bump into you? Shake your hand?

Do you see how many different images you can get from a single line of a song, as a listener? Can you see how many things you as a singer can create from a single line in a song? I learned to do this in my acting classes. As an actor you have to make definite decisions about such details or your character will be flat, with no substance. There will be no character. The same is true for a singer and his or her communication. No one will believe you if you don't know and mean what you're singing about.

Acting classes from a qualified teacher will help you develop skills such as those discussed above. And, by the way, the same information contained earlier in Chapter 2, "How to Select a Vocal Coach," applies when you're selecting an acting coach. If you need to review that material, please don't hesitate. Simply apply the same basic questions and modify them to suit an acting coach.

One final, important note: If the acting teacher you study with can't help you connect your singing with the acting, find a teacher who can.

MOVEMENT AND DANCING

How do I know if I should take a dance class? If you feel awkward onstage and don't feel comfortable moving your body around, then take dance lessons or take a class in some kind of movement. If you plan on going into one of the more dance-oriented styles of singing, then you *must* learn how to dance. As a matter of fact, you should keep up on the latest dances. Watch shows like SOUL TRAIN that introduce the new dances. I know some singers who have been passed over in auditions because they couldn't dance.

Many kinds of dance classes, both private and group, are available. Some of the styles of dance you can learn are tap, hip hop, jazz, ballroom, and even belly dancing. You can also take a gymnastics class. All of these activities will help you feel more comfortable and confident about moving your body around onstage.

Again, apply the same questions and observations I suggested for selecting a vocal coach to choosing a dance teacher. By all means watch how dance teachers handle their students. Are they abusive to them—do they make them look bad in front of the class? If a particular teacher only pays attention to the best dancers in the class and the rest have to just "keep up," then don't study with that teacher. A teacher with that kind of attitude won't be there for you and chances are you won't learn anything. Of course, if you're an incredible dancer, then maybe that teacher would be right for you. But if you're that incredible, you might not need a teacher! Anyway, you get the idea.

THE PERFORMANCE

Choosing Songs for the Show

If you're in a cover band (a band that plays songs and hits released and made popular by other artists), your only limitation in song choices is making sure you get songs you like to sing that will make the audience dance. When I was in a cover band, I would pick the best and most current songs off the radio. If the original key is a bad key for you, you may have problems. But if you and the band can really play the song well, you can probably get away with changing the key. Remember, though, you have to really sing the song well, because the audience will compare you to the original artist. One alternative to changing a key is to have one of the other band members sing the song—that is, if he or she can really do a great job with it!

One of the most successful things I did with my band was to make up our set list (the list of songs for the show) with three songs in a row that were very danceable, followed by a slow ballad. Our sets were usually 45 minutes long and we would do four sets a night, which worked out to be roughly 30 songs a night. Yes, you *do* have to know a lot of songs, and you have to keep learning new ones all the time to stay current. You can throw in some classic oldies too, because familiar songs always go over well.

In my opinion, singing in a cover band is the best thing singers can do to improve their performance skills. Most of the young artists coming up today have absolutely no stage experience, haven't the slightest idea of how to handle an audience, and therefore have no stage presence. They have spent their entire singing career up to that time in a recording studio, and when they emerge to perform in front of a room full of record company executives or a regular audience, they get terrible stage fright. Consequently, their performance suffers. There was a time when bands were scouted and signed from the live shows they played and the only way to get signed was playing out. Working with a cover band is like practicing every time you perform and getting paid for it. You'll perfect your mic technique and learn how to work with an audience, the band—and so much more!

If you don't put together your own band, locate a casual band or Top 40 band and audition for it. Casual bands usually work weekends for weddings, bar mitzvahs, and similar gigs. Top 40 bands do covers in dance clubs, etc.

Performing Original Material

If you're in a band that plays original music, that's good too, as long as you're going out and performing in front of audiences. If you're a "garage band" (a band that only plays and rehearses in a garage or in private, not in front of an audience), then you won't get the necessary stage and live performance experience you need to develop your craft.

When you're making up your set list for an original band, keep in mind that you are playing music the audience has never heard before. Try to arrange the songs so as to get the attention of the audience with the first song. It should be your strongest song and it would be better if it is an up-tempo tune rather than a ballad. You should finish your set with an up-tempo song, too. I'll always remember what one of my first managers told me: Always start and end strong. He was definitely right about that. Another of his tips was to make sure you didn't make a mistake on the first song or the last one because the audience will "always remember the first mistake and never forget the last one."

As for the remainder of the set, you don't want to mix up your audience by alternating fast and slow songs one after the other. You should put at least one or two ballads in your set for sure, but make sure they are spaced far enough apart so the set won't drag.

Be aware of how the audience responds to each song—and what their mood is. They will give you an indication of what songs they like best and whether the set flows well from song to song. If it seems like you're losing their attention, then change the order of the songs. It's OK to do that in the middle of a set when you're trying out new material on a group of people. Putting a song in the wrong place can kill the mood of an audience.

If you've changed the order of songs and the audience is still not responding, then you need to make sure you're doing your job communicating the song. Maybe you're not being heard very well due to a poor sound system, or perhaps the song is not a strong one. You get the idea—observe what the audience response is and fix whatever isn't working.

Handling Energy Problems During Performances

If you are the only vocalist in the band and find yourself running out of steam in the middle of the set, there are several things you can do, depending on the cause. This can happen for reasons having to do with your health, which I will cover in more detail in Chapter 5, "Staying Healthy and Sane." But for now I'll list a few other common causes for lack of energy and what you can do about it:

1. **Lack of sleep.** Make sure you get enough sleep the night before a show.

2. **Eating problems.** These are caused by a bad diet, eating too much before the show, not eating enough before the show, eating too close to showtime. If you're used to eating fast food, you should begin eating more healthful foods that actually give you some nutritional value. Don't stuff yourself before a show. Eat just enough food to give you energy, but not enough to bog yourself down. By all means don't go on stage hungry, as you will have no energy or fuel. Singing is hard work and you need energy. On the other hand, never, ever make the mistake of eating a big meal just prior to showtime. You should give your body a chance to digest the food—at least two to three hours—or more if you've had a big meal.

3. **Illness.** Frequently it's turned out that when my students were feeling very tired and had no energy to perform, they got sick right after the show. You can keep yourself healthier and do a lot to prevent illness by following the hints in Chapter 5.

4. **Too many songs bunched together that demand heavy vocals.** The songs may not be paced correctly for your needs. Try to space the songs containing heavy vocal parts throughout

the set so as to give your voice a little rest. Also, if your voice is beginning to tire during a song, you can let one of the band members take a solo.

5. **Out of shape, not enough exercise.** Everyone who plans on having a career as a vocalist should be working out. You'll have a very hard time on the road if you're out of shape.

6. **Incorrect vocal technique.** Make sure the vocal technique you use gives you all the skills you will need to do anything you want with your voice— consistently, without strain. You should be able to apply your vocal technique to your singing without sounding like that's what you're doing! If your vocal technique doesn't permit you to do that, then you need to find a technique that does.

Here is one more piece of advice concerning points 3 and 4 above. If you are sick with a cold or similar illness and still have to sing, but your voice feels weak, there are several things you can do to compensate. Work the mic more—in other words, take greater advantage of the mic techniques discussed in Chapter 6 to lessen the strain on your voice. In the section "What's Mic Technique?" you will learn how to "kiss the mic." You can use this technique on the parts of the song that are weak. Also take a break and let the band do an instrumental. Don't put all the most vocally challenging songs at the end of the set, and don't put them all together one right after the other. Instead, spread them out.

What If I Get Bored Singing the Same Songs all the Time?

If you find yourself getting bored with your songs, then you are not singing the song newly each time, as though you've never done it before. This is a very important thing to know. Most of the people in the audience have probably never heard the song before and are hearing it for the first time. So you have to sing it like you're singing it for the first time, with all the passion and energy you had then—not like the it's the 500th time! The song itself is not boring. *You* are bored because you're thinking about how many times you've sung the song. But hopefully you'll get a record deal, record your song, and it will be around forever, with you singing it! If your songs are big hits, people will want to hear them over and over again, and you'll have to sing them. If you decide to become a Broadway singer and you're fortunate enough to be the lead in a hit musical with a five-year run, you'll have to sing the same songs six days a week and twice on Saturday and Sunday—for five years!

Know Your Audience

This is a very important part of your job. You wouldn't book yourself in a place where the audience was expecting to hear country music if you were an R&B, hip-hop act, would you? Sometimes if you have an agent who isn't doing his job booking you into the right places, mistakes can happen. It happened to me—*once*. I was sent to a very small town with my band, and in this town there were people who had very different ideas about certain ethnic groups. My band consisted of two Jewish guys, two African Americans and one Asian. We played R&B dance music, but the audience was only used to songs like "Your Cheatin' Heart." We were stuck there for what seemed like an eternity, even though it was only two weeks over the Christmas and New Years holidays. It was the worst experience of my life!

In a similar vein, one of my students told me a story of how a Caucasian pop band was sent to an African-American area of town to perform immediately after the civil unrest in Los Angeless. In the first place, it was in bad taste for the organization to send the group there at that time. Secondly, the group was not well received because they didn't know how to communicate to that type of audience.

You have to make sure you know what kind of audience you are expected to perform for. You have to know the reality of your audience—in other words, the things they like. As an artist, it's important for you to know who *your* audience is. You should know the age group you want to reach and what kind of music appeals to it so that you can focus your music to it.

The Mood of the Audience

When you're doing a live show, it is a very good idea to know what kind of mood your audience is in before you go out. Why? I'll give you an example from the experience of another of my students. This student was given the opportunity to perform "Amazing Grace" for her church. She was very happy to be performing and cheerfully sang the song to a packed house. When the song was over, to her surprise, she barely got any kind of response. Afterwards, in our lesson, I worked with her on the different emotions the song could be performed in. We agreed that grief was the appropriate emotion for a performance of that song in front of that audience. The following Sunday she performed the song again, this time creating the emotion of grief, and got a standing ovation. And the emotion was the only thing she changed in the song!

You don't always have to make drastic changes in your music for each audience. You should know how to feel the audience out to see how they will respond to a song you plan on performing. If the audience seems like it needs a kick in the pants to get them going, then do an up-tempo song instead of a ballad. Or choose a song that is close to where that audience lives emotionally. This will get their attention. So what if you have to alter the order of your set! Once you get their attention, you can resume the regular order. It's much better to have changed the order, got the audience's attention, and communicated with a lot of impact, than to have stayed in strict order and bombed!

When creating your act or show, take the audience on an emotional journey and they will have a great time and never forget you. And that's *really* how you get a record deal and eventually sell lots of records!

More on Controlling Your Audience

When you get really good at being able to read the emotions of your audience, you will easily be able to control it and never have to be adversely affected by an audience out of control. This is vital. Begin to observe individuals and audiences to try to determine what emotion they're manifesting. Practice doing this wherever you happen to be. Is your audience bored, angry, antagonistic? When you are able to determine what mood the audience is in, you will be able to communicate appropriately to them and control them.

In learning this myself, I experimented on every audience I sang to. If I wanted the crowd to dance, I'd pick a certain type of song and they would dance. If I wanted them to sit down and listen to me sing, I'd do another kind of song. If there weren't a lot of people in the room and it was late and the guys in the band and I wanted to go home, I'd pick another type of song and the few people who were there would leave! I knew I was really good when I did a song to make some people leave, then changed my mind about them leaving—and they stayed! That's when I realized I was really in control of my audience.

It is interesting that many singers I've spoken with say that Los Angeles audiences are among the toughest for any singer. They exhibit an antagonistic, "show me" attitude toward artists until they prove themselves. If you are faced with this type of audience, you first have to recognize the audience's predominant emotion, and then come at them with the same emotion in your choice of songs as well as your performance. Usually an up-tempo song will get their attention and make them listen. You would never do a ballad with an antagonistic audience unless you were a Luther Vandross with his amazing ability to control his audiences. On the other hand, this doesn't mean you would "disrespect" your audience, which would be bad stage manners. However, you would reflect that emotion in your songs.

I remember a show where the audience was drugged-out, drunk, unruly and throwing things onstage. They were chanting the name of the headliner, who was obviously late and hadn't even arrived yet at the venue. I was ceremoniously thrown to the wolves—I was told that I had to perform for this audience to kill time until the headliner arrived. I used my knowledge of audience emotions to get the audience's attention, and I did it with a song the audience had never even heard before! In fact, I mesmerized them with that song. By its end, the entire audience of about 20,000 people was singing along with me.

These experiences have helped me learn that it is my intention to put a certain kind of emotion into each of my songs, along with my intention to affect the audience a certain way, that makes them respond the way I want them to. You can learn to control audiences the same way.

Talking to the Audience

Sometimes a vocalist will go into a fright because he or she has to talk to the audience and doesn't know what to say. This phenomenon usually occurs when you have stage fright and don't feel totally comfortable onstage. Well, remember, the audience is made up of people. Speak to them the same way you speak to anyone. Also, you should know that you don't have to talk to the audience all the time. Usually a singer will think that because there's nothing going on onstage, or there is a musical break, or some technical problem has to be handled, they *have* to talk. If you choose to talk it's OK. If you choose not to talk, it's OK too. The more comfortable you are onstage, the more at ease you will feel about just being there doing nothing. You can have something prepared to say if you feel better about it, but I feel that that usually comes across as unnatural.

Lip-Syncing

Lip-syncing is when you pantomime the song. There is a real art to doing it well. I'm sure you've seen artists on TV who look like they're in a cheap monster movie and their lips don't match the words of the song. That's bad lip-syncing! It takes a lot of practice to get so good at it that you really look like you're singing the song live.

You're most likely to be required to lip-sync when you're shooting a video or taping a TV show. Since the invention of the DAT (digital audio tape), a singer will often sing live to a track. If the singer isn't that good, the record company or manager will have the artist lip-sync. But a really good singer will try to sing live to the recorded track, which includes instruments and background vocals. There are sometimes other reasons that the singer isn't able to sing live to a track and must lip-sync—there may not be enough time to do a sound check at the venue, or the set-up may not be ideal to make the vocalist sound good. It can sometimes be to your advantage to lip-sync in a situation where you may not sound good because of technical problems with equipment.

When I have to lip-sync, as has occurred with a video and a movie, I actually sing along with the song instead of only mouthing the words, because I feel more emotion that way. Usually I don't have to worry about making mistakes because I'm doing my own material. I know what and how I sing certain parts of the song. As long as the mic is not on, there should not be a problem singing along.

As I mention in the section "What's a Sound Check" in Chapter 6, whenever you are going to do a track date (a gig where you sing to pre-recorded tracks minus vocals) or have to lip-sync, bring your accompaniment on a DAT, not a cassette tape. Not all tape players play at the same speed, and it could throw your performance off.

EXERCISES

1. Think of a time when you were on stage singing and experienced any of the distractions or mental phenomena listed at the beginning of this chapter. Add to your list anything you experienced that isn't mentioned on my list. Next, recall how successful your performance was and how you felt after the show.

2. Do Exercises 1 and 2 in the "How To Handle Stage Fright" section above.

3. Go to a Karaoke club and practice singing in front of the audience.

4. Practice doing some of the stage manners exercises recommended in this chapter.

5. Go and audit (listen in) on some acting classes that have been recommended to you. Once you find an acting coach that you feel comfortable with, start the class. Be sure to apply the information from Chapter 2 on selecting a vocal coach to choosing your acting coach.

6. Apply the information discussed in the section, "How to Make a Song Real to the Audience," to one of your songs. As you do this, note how the song changes and how you feel about singing it.

7. If you feel confident about your dancing and can hold your own on the dance floor, you probably don't need lessons. If, on the other hand, you feel awkward, locate a good teacher and begin dance lessons.

8. If you have not done so already, check to see if your songs are in the right key for you and suit you and not another member of the band. If you find a song that is better for someone else in the band, pass it along.

9. If you're a studio singer and have never performed in front of an audience, begin performing to live audiences—now! Do it a lot!!!

10. If you're in an original band and you're not getting the response you want or think you should be getting from the audience, try changing the set list. If the audience response doesn't change after you do this, take a look at your communication skills. Make the necessary corrections.

11. If you are bored with any of your songs, apply the information in the section called "What If I Get Bored Singing the Same Songs all the Time?" Take note of what happens to you and your audience when you apply this data at your next performance.

12. The next time you attend the performance of a live band, see if you can spot a singer who is bored while singing. What kind of an effect does this cause on you—how does it make you feel?

13. While attending a concert or other live performance, see if you can spot the mood of the audience before the show. Watch the reaction of the crowd as the singer sings each song. What mood is the audience in at the end of the show? Hopefully the audience will be elated and feeling good.

14. Before you begin your next performance, see if you can spot what mood your audience is in. Then note what kind of mood they are in when you're done. If the audience is in the mood you wanted them to be in by the end of your show, you did your job. If not, then you need more work on the subjects covered in this chapter.

15. When planning your next performance, find out what kind of audience you are expected to entertain and make sure you're the right band for that audience.

16. If you don't feel comfortable talking to an audience, review the section in this chapter called "Stage Manners."

17. Use a mirror to practice your lip-syncing technique. Continue working at it until it looks and feels natural.

18. Now book some shows of your own. It could be a friend's party or college party or concert. Perhaps a relative will be having a party and wants to provide some entertainment. Next, book a paid, professional gig for yourself. Do this a lot!

Chapter 5

Staying Healthy and Sane

HOW DO DRUGS AFFECT SINGING?

Without a doubt doing drugs of any kind is the worst thing you can do for yourself physically and spiritually.

Smoking grass burns your vocal cords, and the smoke in your lungs limits your ability to breathe properly. As I mentioned earlier, 80% of singing is breath control. So it's really stupid to smoke grass or anything else if you're serious about singing—and I'm using the word "stupid" intentionally. Sure you can say you know someone who smokes and they sing just fine and it doesn't affect them. Perhaps they do sing just fine, now. But what about in a few years? And have you ever thought about just how much better they would sound if they didn't smoke at all?

Illegal drugs like grass, cocaine, and all the rest affect your perceptions and your ability to hear music correctly and make the correct decisions about your singing. I remember in my early days of music when the guys in my band and I would smoke grass and then go into the studio to record. During the sessions we would listen to what we were doing and thought it sounded great. The next day when we were no longer high, we would listen to what we had done in the studio and hear how awful it sounded. We would wonder how we could possibly have thought it sounded good. But no one thought it could possibly have been the drugs that were affecting our judgment. We wasted thousands of dollars and lots of studio time recording songs that sounded like garbage!

I was even stupid enough to try cocaine. But that didn't last long because it numbed my vocal cords so that I couldn't feel what was happening with them when I was singing. I valued my voice too much to risk losing it, so I didn't continue. Shortly after that I started getting into yoga. Since the guys in the band always smoked a joint in the morning and didn't want to wait until I finished my yoga exercises, I was left out of the daily ritual. Believe me, it was impossible to try to stand on my head if I was loaded! Eventually I started to feel really good, had more energy and sang better. I finally figured out that smoking grass was harmful to my health and I was better off without it.

When a new student comes into my studio loaded, I always spot it. I had a guy who was loaded on cocaine and didn't think I could tell. But people on drugs have dispersed attention and are not focused—in short, they act drugged. Before the end of any lesson with someone who is loaded, I make sure they know I will not teach them if they continue to do drugs. This is because people who use drugs are too difficult to teach—they are not really "there" or able to focus their full attention on the lesson.

Drugs affect the body negatively in many ways, including destroying brain cells, weakening the immune system, and distorting your perceptions—usually for the worse. They cloud the mind so you can't think clearly. Additionally, since people who do drugs usually don't take care of themselves, they are sick a lot. Spiritually, drugs lower your self esteem, reduce your sense of responsibility, and reduce your ability to achieve your goals.

Think about how many artists' lives are destroyed and ended through drug abuse, and do yourself a favor: If you're considering starting, think again! If you do drugs now, stop. And if you don't do drugs, that's great—you have already made the best decision for yourself!

There are so many books and so much information you can read on the subject of the dangers of drug abuse, I don't think it's necessary to go into any more detail about it. My intention here has been to let you know my personal experiences with drug use, my experiences with singers who have used drugs, and my observations as to how harmful drug use is to a vocalist.

If you have been involved with drugs and need help, I strongly recommend the Narconon®[11] program, which is available in many parts of the U.S.—it is completely unlike any other rehab program and has by far the highest success rate of any method or organization. And even better, Narconon's graduates have the lowest reversion rate of any rehab program in existence. Narconon's telephone number from anywhere in the world is (800) 468-6933. The Los Angeles area telephone number is (213) 962-2404.

EXERCISE AND DIET

If you plan on having a career as a professional singer or recording artist—*especially* if you tour—you should exercise regularly. Touring is so stressful and strenuous that you won't make

---

11   ©1997. All rights reserved. Narconon is a trade and service mark owned by Association for Better Living and Education and used with its permission.

65

it unless you're in good health. In bygone years, instead of following a healthful diet and exercising, many artists, with the assistance of unethical doctors, took drugs to keep themselves going—uppers to keep them up and downers to make themselves sleep. This was and still is a sure road to eventual ruined health and, sometimes, death.

Many times while on tour you will be traveling from city to city, not getting enough sleep between one day's concert and the next day's sound check. If you're doing this from one end of the country to the other through different time zones, or from one country to another, a lot of stress will be placed on your body and your resistance can be lowered. Often, when you're on tour and promoting your record, you will be asked to do radio interviews and TV appearances at 6:00 a.m. How will you ever manage this kind of brutal schedule, not to mention avoid illness, if you're not healthy and in good shape?

If you have a lousy diet, improve it! Find a diet that suits your needs so your immune system doesn't weaken, predisposing you to illness. There are many books out on different kinds of healthful diets. And when I say diet, I *don't* mean depriving yourself of food. I'm talking about supplements (called micronutrients) and food (called macronutrients) that keep you healthy and don't make you overweight.

Here are some of my own successful actions: I never eat red meat (beef, pork or lamb), and rarely consume dairy products. I strongly recommend that you not eat dairy products for two weeks prior to a recording date or show. Also, *drinking milk is the worst thing you can do to your voice.* It will produce tons of mucus and congestion—especially when you have a cold. If you can't do without milk, try soy milk, rice milk or goat's milk—they are more readily digestible and are not mucus-forming. I follow these dietary guidelines because I have extremely high expectations for my voice and always want to be in top condition when I sing. Meat and dairy products interfere with my ability to maintain that condition.

How do meats and dairy products interfere with your singing and your health? All of them, when ingested, make your body toxic. A cold is nature's way of "cleaning house," or flushing the toxins from your system. When your body is very toxic, it lowers your resistance and makes you vulnerable to all sorts of viruses and infections. Have you ever wondered why cold and flu season arrives with the holidays? It's because for most of us it's party time, and besides eating everything in sight, we don't get enough sleep. This weakens the immune system to the point that any virus can attack you. Then, before you know it, bang! You're sick and your voice is gone.

One additional caution. If you have circumstances in your life that harm your spiritual well-being, such as people who are critical or negative toward you, you can also open yourself up to getting sick or acquiring even worse problems.

The remedies for illnesses and throat problems which follow are invaluable for those times when it's a little too late for prevention.

REMEDIES FOR ILLNESSES AND THROAT PROBLEMS

Over the course of my career as a vocalist and vocal coach, I've taken the time to find many ways to handle sore throats, laryngitis and colds. I've used every kind of natural remedy you can imagine and many of my students have sent me remedies that have worked for them. This section is full of information you can use to defeat many of the symptoms and illnesses that you may encounter. Much of this material is taken from articles I've written for magazines and newsletters.

As you will see, there is a lot of information. I've included it because a lot of it has worked well for me. Also, there is always something new and better coming along, so I keep my eyes open for effective new methods and remedies. You will discover, however, that some of these remedies may seem to conflict with each other. Well, believe me, it's no secret that the field of health care is full of contradictory data! What works for one person won't for another. So the best advice I can give you is to suggest that you try each of these remedies and see which of them work best for *you*.

Natural Remedies

You have a concert or studio session to do, you wake up, and you've got a sore throat that's so bad you can barely talk. What do you do now? I frequently get desperate phone calls from students in this very predicament. What follows are all the remedies that have been effective for my students and me. It's my policy not to recommend anything I haven't tried myself. Since everyone's system is different, you may respond to these remedies differently, so I've given you several options.

Sore Throat. A few years back, I woke up with a sore throat, and by the afternoon I'd completely lost my voice. I was due to leave town that Sunday for a major concert. I made an appointment with my doctor, who believed in treating illness with vitamins. She gave me a vitamin B-12 shot and an intravenous dose of vitamin C. I had my voice back the next day, and by the time of the concert, it was as though I'd never had a problem. Another remedy is to gargle with warm water and epsom salts for five minutes, three times a day (two tablespoons in a glass of warm water). It kills all the bacteria and viruses and works very quickly.

Cold. One day when Billy Sheehan, bassist for the platinum act Mr. Big, came in for his lesson, he warned me not to get too close because he'd just had some raw garlic. I asked why he'd done that, and he said that whenever he felt he was coming down with a cold, he'd crush a fresh garlic clove and swallow it with vegetable juice, continuing to take it two to three times a day until the symptoms were gone. He said it works only if you start *the instant* you feel yourself coming down with a cold. I tried it the next time I was coming down with a cold, and it really did work! I usually take it with carrot juice.

Cold, Chest Congestion, Cough. I was preparing to showcase for a number of record companies and managers and was under a lot of stress and not getting enough sleep. Two days before the showcase I got a cold. Congestion in my chest was making me cough uncontrollably and I lost my voice. My doctor was out of town and couldn't be reached. So I found some new remedies. The first one was given to me by one of my associate teachers at the School of the Natural Voice, Sheila Knight: Mix with hot water the juice of one lemon, a tablespoon of honey, and as much cayenne pepper as you can stand. Drink it. I drank it, and boy, did it clear up my head and chest!

But I didn't stop there. In a book called *Fresh Vegetable and Fruit Juices,* by N.W. Walker, which is available at most health food stores, I found perhaps the most intense remedy yet. In a vegetable juicer, grind, but don't press, $\frac{1}{4}$ pint of fresh horseradish. Discard the juice. When the pulp is ground to the consistency of a sauce, mix it with the juice of one lemon. Take $\frac{1}{2}$ teaspoon twice a day between meals. This will dissolve mucus from your sinus cavities and other parts of your body. By the way, I highly recommend that you read this book to gain a better understanding of caring for your body with fresh juices.

Sinus Problems. An ear, nose and throat specialist named Dr. Demeter recommended two natural herbal remedies for one of my students who suffered from a chronic mucus/dripping sinus problem. She had had a constant sore throat from this condition, and these herbs worked very well. They are called Song of the Nightingale (also good for throat and lungs) and Pe Min Kan Wah. I've used them myself and keep a supply on hand. You can write to Dr. Demeter, E.N.T., at 1370 Foothill Blvd., La Canada, California 91011. His telephone number is (818) 952-1155.

Lung/Bronchial Congestion. The morning after performing in a smoke-filled room, I found that the cigarette smoke and lack of oxygen had taken their toll on my lungs. I got something called Eucalyptus Compound and started taking it in the afternoon. By that evening all the congestion in my chest was gone. You can send for Eucalyptus Compound at Simplers Botanical Co., Box 39, Forestville, California 95436, telephone number (707) 887-2012. Readers located in the Los Angeles area can purchase this and the above remedies at *The Daily Planet* store, 4342½ Tujunga Boulevard, Studio City, California 91604, telephone (818) 752-8000; fax (818) 752-3054; e-mail Dplanet@ad.com. Ask for Kathy Beekman and tell her Gloria Rusch sent you. The Daily Planet store will ship UPS anywhere.

Cold and Flu Prevention. I've saved the best for last. A friend of mine told me about a tea that builds up your immune system so that you simply don't get colds or flu—especially if you maintain healthy eating habits! I began taking it and went through a very rough flu season without even a trace of illness, although at least ten of my students were ill and I was in close contact with them. The tea is called Essiac formula and is available now at many health and nutrition stores.

Hangover Prevention: Take vitamin B1 before bed (with a little food) if you've had too much alcohol.

One additional note: If you get laryngitis, don't *ever* make the mistake of trying to sing. Drink the Essiac tea twice a day and relax until it goes away. It's just not worth prolonging the laryngitis.

Additional Hints for Prevention

1. During the holidays, double up on everything you take to build up your immune system. That time of year is when most people seem to get sick with illnesses such as colds, flu, bronchitis, etc.

2. Make sure you have a good source of fiber to clean your colon out. If you indulge in holiday foods and drinks that you don't normally indulge in during the rest of the year, your body will become toxic. Ever notice how much stuff comes out of you when you get a cold or the flu? Your body naturally wants to clean itself out. The best way to do that is to give itself a cold or if it's really toxic, get the flu.

Since we're really into being healthy, some additional data you should have concerns the colon. If your colon is clean you are less likely to get sick. Virtually every book on nutrition I've read says that most of the problems we have with illness are a result of a toxic colon. Another benefit of having a clean colon is that you absorb more nutrients from your food and supplements. My husband and I recently did a three-month cleanse that was truly amazing. The program is called the Awareness program. And it was as simple as taking three herb products called Experience, Harmony and Clear. My overall well being and my health have improved incredibly. For more information contact Marc Fett (818) 848-9022.

3. The most recent supplements I have used that I find work extremely well come from a company called Mannatech. These supplements have really boosted my immune system. Since starting with these products, I have made it through two seasons of flu without getting the flu (and *without* a flu shot)! You can call (800) 218-4469, Reference #155011, for more information on the Mannatech products.

4. Drink lots of *fresh* juices. I'm partial to a combination of carrot, parsley, beet and cucumber juice mixed together. Also drink *lots* of distilled water. An excellent book on the benefits of water is *Your Body's Many Cries for Water*, by F. Bathmanghelidj, M.D.

5. Eat a little healthful food before you go out so you don't overindulge. If you normally eat healthful foods during the rest of the year, try to eat as healthfully as you can during the holidays.

6. If you're around somebody sick and touch something they touch, wash your hands before you eat something or touch your eyes. If you can, use an anti-bacterial soap.

Here are additional remedies that have worked for me:

1. **Natural Herb Loquat Flavored Syrup Beverage.** This is a Chinese cough syrup that helped me with a cough. It was a little intense at first, really thick. So I used 2 teaspoons of it to sweeten a cup of eucalyptus tea. The Chinese name for it is King To, Nim Jiom Pie Pa Koa. I used it and it worked very well. This product is available in the Los Angeles area at the Daily Planet Store mentioned previously.

2. **Echinacea Baptisia**

3. **Friar's Balsam**

4. **Cyclone Cider**

5. **Zinc lozenge**

6. **Vitamin shots or I.V.** I went to the doctor and got an I.V. of vitamin C and B complex—a pint of fluids full of vitamins. I felt much better and had a lot of energy afterwards.

7. **Acupuncture.**

8. **Camocare.**

9. **Satori Vocal Restore.**

10. **Peroxide and Lemon Juice.** Put 1 oz. of hydrogen peroxide and 1 oz. lemon juice with salt in warm water, and gargle three times daily.

11. **Sugar.** If you have a serious cough, plain old sugar is a natural cough suppressant.

12. **Cough Drops.** I wanted to see for myself which cough drop worked the best, so I got the four most recommended to me by students and two that were advertised on TV:

    (a) Ricola
    (b) Fisherman's Friend
    (c) Janet Zand Herbal Lozenge
    (d) Halls

Out of the above four, Halls worked the best for me. But by all means you should do your own testing, because people's bodies respond in different ways to the same remedies.

Finally, I made sure I got plenty of sleep and didn't talk for three or four days.

Thanks for the above remedies go to Sisu Rankin, who generously shared many of her successful actions on the subject with me.

Remember, I'm telling you about remedies that have worked for me, for my family, and for my friends. I am by no means suggesting that I am an expert in the field of medicine. You should seek medical help when the need arises, and use your common sense and your own judgment. I'm a professional vocalist and vocal coach with years of experience overcoming the same problems you may be having. I'm sure many of you have also discovered your own special methods, as there are many effective remedies out there. If any of the information here is helpful to you, I'm glad—and, if you've used any other natural remedies successfully, please feel free to contact me about them.

How to Handle Vocal Nodes

As I mentioned in Chapter 2, vocal nodes do not necessarily mean you have to have surgery. You can handle nodes by resting your voice for a few weeks or longer. You must stop talking for at least one week, followed by no singing for several weeks. During this period, using your hand, massage the throat with astringent. Then, using a dry washcloth, whisk over the area. These things should be done at least once a day. Also, gargle with vinegar and warm water twice a day (a tablespoon of vinegar to a cup of water), and drink licorice root tea as often as you want. Don't drink cold water or beverages. Then, as soon as you can (when your voice has been repaired), change your vocal technique. Any vocal exercises you do should begin very slowly and you should be careful not to force the voice.

Singing and PMS

PMS (Premenstrual Syndrome) can sometimes have an effect on your singing voice, causing it to feel tight and closed up. You may even have difficulty singing some high notes that you ordinarily would not not have the slightest problem with. These difficulties are caused by the bloating and swelling of tissue that frequently accompanies PMS. The symptoms are only temporary and usually go away after your period begins.

Some New Discoveries

The latest discoveries I've made in the area of health and preventive care have been through my visits to Los Angeles chiropractor and nutritionist, Dr. Arlo Gordin. Not only did Dr. Gordin introduce me to the ultimate immune system builder (which you can order from him), but he taught me how incorrect alignment of the spine and injuries to your neck can affect your singing. Dr. Gordin has created a seminar just for singers to give them data on care of the voice. I had an opportunity to put the immune system supplements to work and they really delivered what was promised. When everyone else around me was getting the flu, I didn't get sick.

Dr. Gordin has also assembled a great product he calls "Your Nutritional Survival Kit." This survival kit contain supplements for injuries, pain, back problems, musician and sports injuries, auto collisions, building your immune system and detoxification after eating food that doesn't agree with you. If you're on the road and fall victim to any of these problems, the kit provides you with remedies to help get you through it so you can continue to perform.

If you live in Los Angeles, you can contact Dr. Gordin at (213) 436-0303. His office is located at 3535 Cahuenga Blvd. West, Suite 206, L.A. CA 90068. If you're out of town, you can call him and order the Nutritional Survival Kit supplements and the immune system builder, along with information on how and when to use these supplements.

Dr. Gordin also highly recommends the book, *Enter the Zone*, by Dr. Barry Sears. If you're one of the ten million women who've ever had a problem losing weight—especially that last ten pounds that just won't seem to go away—I have found the answer. *Enter the Zone* explains exactly why some people can eat anything they want and never gain weight, yet why others eat very little and blow up like a balloon. The book provides you with a solution to handle this problem, and after trying it and having success with it, I too highly recommend it. *Enter the Zone* is widely available in bookstores and health food stores.

EXERCISES

1. If you're using any of the drugs mentioned in this chapter, STOP! I know you probably think you can't or that it's none of my business. I think it *is* my business to the degree that it's my responsibility to tell you what I know works if you want to give yourself and your career a fighting chance.

2. If you need a more gradual approach to stopping drugs, try not doing any for a week and see how you feel. See how it affects your singing.

3. If you need help, call Narconon. Their telephone number from anywhere in the world is (800) 468-6933. The Los Angeles area telephone number is (213) 962-2404.

4. Start a good exercise program. Set realistic goals for yourself.

5. Find out what nutritional program works best for YOU and make a commitment to stick to it.

6. Using some of the remedies suggested in this chapter, make a singer's "survival kit" for yourself to prevent colds, flu and other illnesses and symptoms that can get in the way of your singing.

7. DRINK LOTS OF WATER DAILY: 8 TO 12 GLASSES A DAY.

CHAPTER 6

WORKING WITH SOUND EQUIPMENT

It is important for you to be familiar with the types and grades of sound equipment you will encounter and to acquire the know-how to use it properly. If you have a good mic, good mic technique, a good P.A. and monitor system, a good sound person, and you do a sound check before your show, you stand a very good chance of having a good show.

THE MICROPHONE

Let's start off with the most basic piece of equipment for a singer, the microphone. The microphone is the primary piece of equipment responsible for the way your voice will sound in most instances of performance. A bad mic can make a singer with a good voice sound really bad. In other words, all mics are not created equal. If you have had the unfortunate task of singing through the house system of a hotel banquet room, you know exactly what I mean. The mic that goes with this system is the kind that is usually attached to a podium, and the speakers are usually in the ceiling. This kind of system was built for speaking engagements only and it is truly a *P*ublic *A*ddress system—which is where the term "P.A." came from.

The next category of mics you should steer clear of are the $25.00 variety. They usually come with the mic and cord connected permanently as one piece. Also steer clear of the mics that come with singing machines. They are OK for use with those machines, but are not adequate for professional shows.

What Mic Should I Buy?

When you're just starting out on your career and need to buy your first mic, start off with something reasonably priced and use it until you become more experienced. Then you will know exactly the sound quality you want to achieve for your voice with the mic. So look for a mic that costs between $75 and $450.

There are so many mics on the market that you could literally go nuts trying to figure out which one is right for you. And after the salesmen get through with you, you could wind up spending too much money for something totally wrong for your needs.

The best overall mic I recommend is the Shure SM 58 (ball type) or SM 57 (non-ball type). Professional sound stages and clubs and other establishments that supply a sound system usually use this brand of mic. They're very rugged and stand up to a lot of punishment. Be aware, however, that outright abuse will damage any piece of good equipment.

You will also have to buy a stand with a clip for the mic as well as the cable (which should be no longer than 25 feet). You should plan on spending about $150 to $225 for the mic plus the clip, stand and cable.

A good investment would also be an XLR female to quarter inch male transformer/adapter to connect to the mixing board. Since most *pro* mics come with an XLR type (three-pin) connector on both ends of the cable, a female XLR-to-quarter inch male transformer/adapter ($20) could save the day because some mixing boards only accept quarter inch male connectors.

A line of AKG mics is available in the same price range that is also very high quality. I personally prefer the Shure because the AKG mic puts more of an edge or bright (sharp, high) sound in my voice whereas the Shure gives me a warmer sound. As I've become more experienced and had the opportunity to hear my voice through various systems and mics, I've learned which ones give my voice the sound I like. Experience will give you the same ability to decide which mic is best for your voice.

Here are some more mics that I recommend, although some of them cost more than the two already mentioned: Audix OM 5; Audix OM 6; Beyer M500; Shure Beta 58 and 57, which are updated versions of the SM58 and SM57 with more gain and less feedback potential.

I suggest that when selecting your mic, you go around to a few music equipment stores. By all means, don't be afraid to ask questions. Try out various mics through one of their systems. You may prefer a brighter sound for your own voice.

What About Wireless Mics?

I'm sure you've seen many of the professional singers using wireless mics. Those can be very expensive for a beginning singer. But if you're well off with no budget problems, or you are at the point in your career at which you can afford to spend $2,000 for a wireless, by all means go for it.

You have to be careful when selecting a wireless mic. If you get one that doesn't have a strong signal or one that doesn't have a lot of switchable channels for avoiding interference from other frequencies in your area, you could wind up with a police call or trucker interrupting your love ballad! Or the sound could deteriorate and turn into a horrible loud buzz. So a cheap wireless isn't worth the trouble it can cause. Also be aware that there are two frequencies these systems run on—UHF (Ultra High Frequency) and VHF (Very High Frequency). VHF tends to have more interference than UHF.

When you get into a wireless system, you also have to buy a receiver as well as a transmitter. Sometimes the transmitter is built into the mic, so you don't always have to buy a body transmitter pack. I'm sure you've seen those transmitter packs on the belts of people on talk shows.

As you've probably figured out by now, getting into a wireless system can get expensive really fast. But I must admit that going wireless is great, because you don't have to worry about what to do with the mic cord, and really good wireless mics make your voice sound incredible.

As a note of caution, keep in mind that when you talk to a salesperson who is trying to make a sale, the "best one" (no matter what type of equipment you're purchasing) will always be the one the salesperson wants you to buy!

Just to put things back into perspective, however, I want to remind you that no matter how much money you spend on a great mic, a great P.A. system, and the best sound person in the business, if you can't sing in tune or you have other vocal problems that need to be handled, there isn't anything that a great system can do to fix it. I can assure you that any incredible system will only tend to magnify the flaws.

What's Mic Technique?

Mic technique is the ability to use the mic properly to make sure you can be heard and to get the best sound out of your voice without distortion. You should know when to back off the mic and when to come in close. We use a term in the industry called "kissing the mic." That's when you put your lips right up on the mic while singing into it. I guess that's one good reason to own your own mic—the screens of my first ones were full of lipstick from times when I had to kiss the mic.

How do you know when to kiss the mic and when to pull it away? If you have to sing a very soft passage in a song, usually you get right up on the mic. When you sing loud you back up or pull the mic away. People with really strong or big voices like Pattie LaBelle pull the mic almost an arm's length away from their mouths when they sing loudly. This is so they don't overload the P.A. system and distort the sound of their voice. The more softly you sing, the closer the mic should be so you can be heard. You should experiment with a mic and see what happens when you sing both loudly and softly. You should also watch someone like Whitney Houston use the mic. Whitney has incredible mic technique and achieves a very good overall balance of sound with her voice.

One other thing to remember is not to yell into the mic. If you do, the person running sound will have a very difficult time mixing your voice with the sound of the band or the music tracks you're singing to. Also, if you're singing too softly or you don't have the mic close enough to your mouth, the mix will be unrealistic and the sound person will have a difficult time balancing you with the band or tracks.

Good mic technique ("working the mic"), then, would be knowing when to kiss the mic and when to back off in order to get the best and most consistent sound.

You should keep a few things in mind about the correct handling of a mic. If the mic is hot (on), never point it towards the monitor or any speaker that your vocal will be put through. It will cause feedback. Feedback is a loud screeching sound that usually hurts your ears—you will never forget it once you've experienced it! Don't cup your hands around the mic unless you're trying to cause feedback. I know some of the younger hip rappers do that because they think it looks good. But the fact is you're a singer, not a rapper, and your voice won't sound good if you do that. As a singer, you want to get the highest quality vocal sound possible.

WHAT'S A MIX?

Getting a good mix on the stage and in the house is what the sound person does to get a good blend between the voice and the instruments, so everything can be heard. All the instruments and vocals are checked separately to make sure there is a good blend of highs and lows in the sound. The bass shouldn't be too boomy and the guitar shouldn't be too thin sounding, and the drums shouldn't overpower everything onstage. The vocals should be heard as well. In short, everyone in the band should be able to hear themselves as well as each other. The audience should also obviously be able to hear everything properly. The house mix, done for the audience, is separate from the stage mix, which is for the performers.

If everything is mixed well and you have a good sound person, then there should be no feedback.

MONITORS

You may wonder how everyone is supposed to hear themselves onstage. Simple—monitors! Monitors are small speakers that are part of the P.A. system. The singer will have one or two monitors that sit on the floor in front of her and are pointed back at her. Since she is behind the main P.A. speakers while she's on the stage, the monitors permit her to hear her voice and anything else she wants at her desired level—exclusive of the level that the audience hears. For some major concerts, monitors are placed at intervals across the entire stage so the singer can hear the vocals anywhere she moves. In most cases, the vocalist hears not only the vocals, but also the band or track. On a professional level (for big concerts and in some concert rooms), each person onstage has his or her separate monitor with a mix tailored to that performer's specific needs.

In the past few years a new kind of monitoring system has come on the market for singers—ear monitors. Yes, these are tiny monitors that fit just inside your ear. I have a pair of them, and I must say they are incredible. They're on the expensive side. I got mine at a bargain for under $1,000. I've priced them more recently and, as of the time of this printing, they can run up around $5,000. I haven't used the high-priced ones, but I'm sure you can find some that work really well for around $1,500. Remember, for these to be remote, you'll also need to have a transmitter and a receiver. If you use a wireless mic, then you have to make sure everything is compatible in terms of frequency.

THE NAMM SHOW

One good way to see all the equipment you'll ever need and more is to keep your eyes open for the NAMM show (the National Association of Music Merchants convention). This is a three-day show that takes place twice a year, once in Los Angeles in mid-January, and once in another major city during the summer. A huge number of musical equipment manufacturers exhibit at the show, and you can see and try out every type of equipment available—literally everything connected to the music industry—including P.A.'s, mics, recording equipment and instruments. There's information galore. Additionally, concerts and clinics with *major* recording artists are held.

NAMM is held primarily for merchants in the music business, such as those who own music stores, recording studios, schools, etc., so it's not open to the general public. But if you have a business card that shows you own a music business, or if you know someone who will lend you their pass for a day, it's well worth it to attend. Most of the musicians who attend are those who endorse products for companies that display their products at the show such as Sony, Yamaha, Gibson, etc.

The NAMM show is announced in music trade magazines like *Music Connection* and *BAM*. If you attend, wear comfortable shoes! I've been going for several years and have never had a chance to see everything. I usually just go to the booths that relate to my field of music.

WHAT'S A SOUND CHECK?

The sound check is probably the single most important thing you can do before a show. Remember the mix? Well, you *mix* the sound at the sound check. This is your chance to get all the levels (correct volume and balance) on the instruments and your voice. It's best to do the sound check a few hours before the show. You don't want to rush through it or be pressed for time. If you rush your sound check, chances are you'll be settling for less than the best possible sound. It's worth all the time spent, even though it can be a long and boring process for a singer because the instruments usually get their levels first.

If it's a big gig, then during the sound check all the musicians are going to be put through the P.A. system, and the equalization (balance of highs and lows), reverb, and echo will be checked. All the added gear the sound technician has brought to enhance the sound of the band, including your vocal sound, must be checked and adjusted. If there is remote gear, then that, as well as any other piece of equipment that is going to be used during your performance, should be checked. The sound technician will also make sure the sound is good in the house or room.

If you're singing to a DAT (digital audio tape), you need to make sure you have the correct program selected. If it's a cassette, then it must be cued to the correct starting place for the song. This, however, is a good place to warn you about the dangers of using cassette tapes. Not all tape players play at the same speed. You could have quite a shock and a very unpleasant experience if you get up onstage and start to sing and the song is in a higher key than you've been practicing it because *this* tape player is faster than yours! If you're playing an instrument to the track as well as singing, you're really in for some problems because you'll have to sing between the two different keys if the track is too fast or too slow. Another problem you will encounter with a cassette is *the more songs you put on a tape, the further off from the correct key the recorded music will be,* because *the tape changes speed as it unwinds.* So, for all these reasons, I recommend you use a DAT when singing live to track. It's a much more accurate and high quality system than a cassette system.

Once all the instruments have been sound checked, it's your turn. You will have to sing and speak into the mic at different levels—usually the same levels you will be singing at. Let the sound person know *exactly* what you need in your monitor—more highs, lows, mids, reverb, etc.—as well as the various instruments or the track you're singing to. Maybe you like more drums and keyboards in your monitor mix. Let the sound person know that. If you don't want any drums in your mix let the sound person know that, too. Don't compromise with how you want your monitor mix to sound. Work at it until *you* are 100% comfortable with the sound. You can be sure each of the musicians will do the same for their own sound.

Once everybody is comfortable with their mix, the entire band will play a song or two. At that point you should sing along and see if you like your mix. Can you hear yourself, or is your voice being lost? If you can't hear yourself, that means you need your voice turned up in your monitor. Almost everyone, including the sound technician, will make adjustments to the sound in their mix during this process. When everyone is pleased with the sound, then sound check is finished.

When it's showtime, recheck your mic to make sure the level hasn't been changed. It's the worst thing in the world to have done a great sound check, then get the surprise of your life when you come back two hours later to discover it's all been tampered with. That's happened to me more times than I care to remember. All you have to do to check the sound is say one little "check" into the mic to see if it's the same as when you left. If you don't want to do it personally, have your sound tech do it.

Something else to be aware of is that in some situations the sound will have to be adjusted once the audience is in the house. The acoustics of an empty room change when the room is full of people. Usually this happens in a big auditorium that is very "live" or resonant, similar to a gymnasium.

If you don't have a sound tech, then you'll have to split the duties of getting a thorough sound check between yourself and the other band members. If you're singing to a track, someone will be there to run the system for you.

The more you know about the workings of the sound system and how to achieve the sound you want, the easier it will be for you to get your voice sounding great at every performance.

WORKING WITH SOUND TECHNICIANS

The relationship you develop with the sound person is very important. After all, that person is responsible for how you will sound to the audience. Always treat the sound tech professionally, but with affinity. If you make an enemy of him, you could sabotage your own show. The last thing you want to do is to make him mad just before you have to sing! You can always fire him if he doesn't do his job or you are not pleased with his work. And, as long as you do your job and have good mic technique, he will absolutely love you. The fact that there are so few singers who actually know what to do with a mic causes sound techs a lot of problems.

SHOULD I OWN MY OWN P.A. SYSTEM?

Each situation is different. If you are a self-contained act and can afford your own P.A. system, and have a vehicle large enough to haul it around in, then by all means go for it. But make sure you don't allow your equipment to be stolen out of your truck or from the club—it's very easy to lose mics and other pieces of equipment this way. On the other hand, there are very few places nowadays that don't have decent systems of their own. I prefer to use the house systems and supplement them if I have to, or bring in my own sound people with their own equipment. That way I don't have to concern myself with anything except my performance because I know it'll be taken care of correctly.

When you become a big superstar like Michael Jackson or Madonna and travel around with your equipment in big semi-trucks, then you will be hauling everything for the show with you, including your set, stage, lights, costumes and road crew ("roadies"), to take care of it for you.

Until you reach that position, you'll either have to do it yourself with your band members, hire roadies, or rely on friends to help you. Some session players have what is known as a cartage company transport their equipment and set it up for the gig. After the gig, the cartage company tears the equipment down and returns it to wherever you tell them. A cartage company can, however, be expensive.

EXERCISES

1. Begin researching a good mic for your personal use for live performances.

2. Practice your mic technique until you perfect it for live and studio gigs.

3. Practice doing a sound check at your rehearsals so that when you are at a real gig you'll be familiar with the level you want for your voice when mixed with the instruments.

4. Research a good set of monitors that suit your particular needs, then purchase them.

5. If you've never hired an experienced, professional sound person to run sound for you, make the investment and hire one for your next important gig. Apply the information given in Chapter 2, "How To Select a Vocal Coach," to locating a good sound person. If you can, attend a gig where you can hear how he or she mixes.

CHAPTER 7

STUDIO SINGING

I offer a recording studio workshop for singers in which I teach all the techniques of working and recording in the studio, all the terminology, how to work with an engineer, which microphone to use, and more. This workshop takes all the first-time jitters and fear out of recording your first demo, and also helps to eliminate time you would waste otherwise by not knowing what to expect when you go into the studio. Because so many singers obviously can't attend my Los Angeles workshop, this chapter was written to give you a good idea of what to expect in the recording studio.

STUDIO TERMS

Included in the glossary at the end of this chapter are terms you are likely to hear when you're in the recording studio. You may not use all of these words, but when you know what the producer and engineer are talking about you'll feel more at ease.

WHAT'S THE DIFFERENCE BETWEEN LIVE SINGING AND STUDIO SINGING?

The first, most obvious thing is that there is no audience for you to relate to in the studio. All the visual and emotional cues you use onstage to get the audience going are useless in the studio, and even more disorienting can be the lack of responses from an audience to in turn give *you* more energy. In some cases you can't even see the producer or engineer. So in the studio, you have to create all the emotion for the song without any feedback from an audience. For these reasons, coming into the studio environment for the first time can be quite a shock to a singer. It really shows you what you're made of.

On the other hand, there are many compensating factors to studio singing. As a studio singer, you have as many chances as you need to get it right—within the budget, of course, because time is money. One thing most singers don't realize before they go into a recording session for the first time is the huge number of elements that go to make up the actual session. So, in addition to all of the technical factors you will learn about in this chapter, the singer must have a professional attitude towards the session. Many people are working very hard and investing a great deal of time and technical expertise in the session. It is vital that you, as the singer, be as prepared and knowledgeable as you can so that everything can come together and run smoothly.

When you hear your voice recorded for the first time, you may not think it sounds like you. Al Jarreau told me that when he first heard his voice recorded, he asked the engineer who *that* was. When the engineer told him it was him, he said, "Oh no, no, no! That wasn't me—I don't sound like that!" This happens because the voice is processed through thousands of dollars of equipment in the studio. Then it is processed again during the mix-down session. Then again when the C.D. is mastered, and another time when it's played over the radio or your own personal boom box or stereo system! As you get more experience, you will become used to how your voice sounds recorded.

The large amount of processing the voice is put through during recording is also the reason that some artists don't sound as good live as they do on their recordings. All kinds of outboard gear (any additional equipment used during the recording session) is used to enhance the vocals in the studio. At one time, as most people are now aware of, the vocals were so "enhanced" that *other people* than the named artists would actually sing on the recordings. But the record companies learned their lesson with the Millie Vanillie scandal and don't do that as much any more.

And just to keep things in perspective, you should realize that this vocal enhancement is also the reason it is almost impossible to make yourself sound exactly like a recorded professional singer as you do record copies. If you try to compare your voice with the voice of a professional singer whose voice has been processed multiple times and decide you don't sound good, you'll be putting yourself down for no good reason.

It is interesting to note that in the early days of recording, singers could really sing and the musicians really played their instruments, as was the case with the early Motown artists. There weren't any computers or sequencing procedures like there are now. Well, guess what? The record companies are again moving towards signing singers who can really sing and don't need enhancing other than the normal overdubs.

WHAT HAPPENS IN A STUDIO SESSION?

The main thing you as a singer are responsible for in the studio is to really create the song so it sounds like you mean every word, concept and emotion—like it's coming from the heart. You have to sell the song you're singing. Since you don't have an audience to feed off of, you have to create *everything* yourself. A record company exec can tell immediately whether you're into the song or not and, once it's recorded, so can record buyers. If you don't really get into the song, then all you'll get on tape is someone who perhaps has a nice voice and sings pleasantly—but no emotion will come across and the song will not communicate. So you have to do all of the above and still sing *in tune*, in the pocket (in the groove and in time with the rest of the band, with emotion, feeling the time), with good phrasing.

For all these reasons, singing for the purpose of recording is much more precise and demanding that singing in live performance. You can see why it's important to have mastered all the fundamentals and basics of singing before you set foot in the studio. There is so much to focus on that if you don't have your voice under control, you'll have a really difficult time. You don't want your first experience in the studio to be an unpleasant one.

In the studio you don't have to sing as hard as you do in a live performance. Your singing should be effortless and without strain. If you strain, it will be heard in the recording. If you can't sing without straining, check to see if the song is in the right key. If it is, but you're still straining, you may need to take some lessons to eliminate the problem.

The mics that are used in a professional studio are very expensive ($2,000 plus) and very high quality. They pick up the sound of *everything!* If you scratch, breathe, or move around, it will be heard. But these mics make your voice sound incredible and you can hear everything your voice does. If your voice is good, it will sound better. But if your voice has flaws, they will be amplified. Make sure that you know how to use the mic. There is usually a wind screen between you and the mic to diffuse your breath to eliminate popping sounds. You should, however, work ahead of time on improving your ability to sing consonants so that you will make as few popping sounds as possible.

Don't wear any jewelry that jingles or clothes that will make sounds as you move—because you are likely to start moving as you really get into your song. Don't wear a watch that has an alarm on it, and if you have a pager or cellphone, leave them in the control room. It would be the worst thing in the world if you were recording a great take and right in the middle of it the alarm on your watch, your pager, or your phone went off. Same thing would go for the charms on your bracelet clinking together!

In most cases, you will also have to refrain from clapping your hands, snapping your fingers, or tapping your feet if you are standing on a wood or other type of hard floor in the vocal booth. Some studios use carpet under your feet to eliminate this problem.

You will be wearing a set of headphones, referred to as "cans." They enable you to hear yourself and the music you will be singing to. You are usually alone in the vocal booth. You may be asked to use only one side of the headphone unit and push the other earpiece to the side of

don't mean your friends —— I'm talking about a real audience of people who don't know you. That means you have to get out and do some performing with your material.

3. **Make sure your songs are in the right key for you.** Your producer can help you with this, too. There's nothing worse than finding out after you've recorded the basic tracks that the songs are in the wrong key. Of course, if you sequence the songs on computer, it's easier to change the key with a simple touch of a button. But I guarantee you will save time if you have the right key worked out beforehand.

4. **Know the correct tempo (time) and rhythm of the song.** If the song is played too fast or too slow, you won't feel it like you should, your performance may be uninspired, and the song won't come out the way you planned.

5. **Sequencing vs. live musicians.** Decide with your producer whether you're going to sequence the entire demo, use some live musicians, or use all live musicians. Keep in mind that once you add live musicians to a sequenced track, you can't change the key unless you're willing to go back and re-record everything.

6. **Make sure you practice the songs.** Don't go into the studio unprepared, as you will waste time and money.

7. **Make at least three copies of the lyrics and music**—one for the engineer, one for the producer, and one for yourself.

8. **Stay healthy and get enough rest.** Combined with a healthy diet and exercise program, sufficient rest will help prevent your getting run down or ill. (For more information on maintaining good health, see Chapter 5.)

9. **Don't drink any alcohol or take any drugs before or during the session.** Alcohol is a drug and, like other drugs, will distort your perception of what the music really sounds like. You should have room temperature distilled water in the studio to drink.

10. **Don't eat any milk or dairy products for about two weeks prior to going into the studio.** This will prevent you from having mucus in your throat while you're singing.

11. **Don't allow anyone in your environment to put any negativity on you or your project.** For example, this could include criticism of any kind, even if subtle, or negative emotions such as anger or hostility. If you feel this coming from anyone, even your producer, get them to knock it off or cut them loose.

12. **Stay focused on what you have to do.** If you have any family problems, bills, or boyfriend or girlfriend problems, park them. Don't bring them into the studio or allow them to interfere with what you have to do.

13. **Warm up your voice before going into the studio.** I usually warm up for about 45 minutes to an hour. Prior to that I vocalize two hours every day for two weeks straight.

14. **Don't overdo it and tire your voice while recording.** Ideally, you shouldn't spend more than three hours recording vocals. After about two hours, the vocal cords start to get tired and don't work as well as they did when you first started singing. If you compare your vocals from the beginning of the session to your vocals after two hours of singing, you'll see what I mean. More often than not a producer will try to go for as long as possible. I've heard of some producers who keep the singer working for hours and hours, and the next day the singer's voice is trashed.

You have to really know your voice and at what point it starts to tire, and the producer must understand and work with you so you don't overwork your voice. When your voice gets tired, you'll start to sing out of tune, have a hard time controlling your voice, and maybe get a little sore. The next thing you'll do is start to force your voice, and the quality of the sound will be different than at the beginning of the session. Be sure to take rests during the actual recording session. The rests actually help your voice last longer.

If you have problems singing a particular line in a song, take a break. This will give you some rest and you'll be able to regroup. When you try the line again after the break, you will usually be able to nail it the first time.

After a few sessions and additional studio experience you'll begin to recognize how to work your voice to get the best out of it.

15. **Find a good recording studio and engineer.** There are so many studios in Los Angeles, you can shop around and get a good price. If you live in an area where there aren't a lot of studios, you may pay a little more. Your producer can help with this area, too. The producer may have a favorite studio or have one of his or her own, as well as have a preferred engineer. You could also get a reference from a musician or singer.

STUDIO MICS AND HEADPHONES

The mic is what's going to pick up the sound of your voice so it can be recorded onto the track, so the higher the mic's quality, the better the recorded sound will be. Many different types of mics are used in recording studios. If you're starting your own little home studio, you can get away with using the trusty Shure SM 58 mic. The really high tech recording studios use expensive, high-tech mics.

The mics I'm most familiar with and which seem to work the best for my voice are the Neumann 467 and the AKG tube. They are quite different from the ones used in live performances and they are much more sensitive. Once again, the more experience you have recording, the better you'll become at recognizing what makes your voice sound the best. Don't shortchange yourself by thinking that you don't have to pay attention to which equipment best suits your voice. Professional studios supply the mics and you will usually have a choice.

As for headphones, the better the quality, the better the sound. Headphones are a very important piece of equipment for you while recording, because they control how you hear yourself. I've used headphones that distort when the level is turned up beyond the capacity of the little speakers inside the earpiece. I've also used good ones that hurt your ears after an hour because they press on your ears. I have my own pair of ear monitors that I sometimes use in the studio instead of the regular headset. But if the studio has a really high quality system, I use the studio headphones. So ask questions, whether you are recording in a professional studio or going to buy a pair of headphones for your own recording studio.

HOME STUDIOS

If you're fortunate enough to have a friend who has a studio, or you personally own your own home studio, then you're very lucky. But unless your home studio is in a soundproof room and you have privacy with no interruptions, and you have a really good mic, you're going to "pay your dues" by recording under less than ideal conditions. You will experience a lot of distractions—the phone ringing, car and airplane sounds, trying to be the engineer/producer/artist at the same time, trying to do punches, friends and neighbors coming over, pets making sounds or demanding attention, roommates, husbands, wives, girlfriends, boyfriends, etc.

None of these things come up at a live gig, so you'll get a lot of experience learning how to record your vocals and you will really appreciate being in a professional studio when the time comes. If you can handle all of that and still come out with a great sounding demo, just imagine how prepared you'll be in a professional studio. But on the up side of home studio recording, you can get some pretty good performances because you're not under the gun to finish by a certain time for financial reasons. The less stress, the greater the opportunity for magic!

YOUR HAT VERSUS THE PRODUCER'S HAT

Finally, I want to make sure you realize that each person who participates in the session has his or her own job, and should be allowed to do it. Your hat is to be THE SINGER. The producer's hat is to be THE PRODUCER. As the vocalist, one of the most important things you need to learn to do is LET THE PRODUCER WEAR HIS HAT! If you both understand what your hats are, and you let each other do them, everything will run smoothly. Most of this book concerns itself with the singer's hat. What exactly is the producer's hat?

The producer hires musicians and background singers, finds the right engineer for the session, mixes the songs and gets you a high quality completed product. The producer is also responsible for getting the project done within budget. When you're in the session, be sure to direct all of your concerns and considerations to him. It is the producer's job to make sure the session runs smoothly and stays on schedule. He should also be someone you can work well with—not a dictator. The producer should be someone you can rely on to get the job done.

I'll give you a perfect example of the artist letting the producer wear his hat. Joe Cocker recorded the song, "You Are So Beautiful To Me." Remember, in the last line of the song, how Joe Cocker's voice breaks up? Well, he didn't like the way his voice sounded there and wanted to do it over. The producer objected and refused to allow him to re-do that line. And as it turned out, that was the best part of the song and according to the producer, made that song the hit that it was. The line was so emotional, it would have been a sin to re-do it.

Another lesson to be learned from the above incident is that in some instances, it's necessary to keep a line containing a technical flaw if it sounds great and really communicates to the listener. This was one of those times. So listen to your producer—he or she may be right sometimes!

Another of my students went into the studio prematurely against my advice and that of her producer. She wasn't technically ready to record, she didn't have control of her voice and didn't have the confidence to pull off what was needed. And she picked a song that was beyond her ability. She wanted to have a session singer come in and do a scratch vocal (a vocal track that is used to cue the musicians—usually not used on the final recording) so she would have a guide to listen to and practice her vocal against. The producer hired professional musicians and background vocalists for the session. The singer he hired for the scratch lead vocal was also a professional session singer.

When it was time for the student to lay her vocal track, she was so intimidated by the level of professionalism of the singers, she couldn't sing. She tried all kinds of tricks, like putting baffles between her and the control room so no one could see her, turning out the lights, and even singing along with the scratch vocal. She insisted I be in the vocal booth with her to coach her through. But none of this was sufficient to get her past her own deficiencies. She then blamed the producer for her inability to sing the song, fired him and got her husband to produce her lead vocal. But even though he was a musician, he did not know how to produce a record. By the end of this fiasco, this student spent thousands of dollars on a demo that turned out to be worthless. The experience was painful for everyone involved, and it cost her a valuable friendship. If she had been willing to confront the fact that she wasn't ready, and if she had been willing to heed the professional advice given her, she could have averted this disaster.

GLOSSARY OF STUDIO TERMS

The following glossary of common recording studio terms was written by Randy Tobin, veteran recording engineer, producer, songwriter, composer and vocalist. The definitions were written in as non-technical a way as possible so as to be easier to understand.

ANALOG - Continuous sound wave; an analog sound wave looks similar to a spaghetti noodle (compare with "digital").

BASIC TRACKS - The individual instruments and vocals, each put down on separate tracks of a multitrack recorder. On a 24-track recorder you can have up to 24 separate tracks. A single track may contain more than one instrument or voice, however. (see Multitrack Recorder)

CANS - Slang for headphones.

COMPRESSION - Automatic volume adjustment (made with a device called a compressor) designed to keep the maximum level of sound from exceeding the recorder's limits. This helps to make vocals more intelligible by raising the average level of the performance (similar to "limiting" but not as drastic).

CONSOLE - The expansive desk-like mixing unit with dozens of knobs and sliders, usually at the center of the control room between the speakers in the studio.

DIGITAL - Sound represented by tiny samples (1/44,000th of a second in length) and stored as computer data (numbers), one after the other. This rough stair-step computer data is smoothed out by special filters called DACs (Digital to Analog Converter) before we hear it.

DOLBY - Originally the name of one of the first pro tape noise reduction systems (named for the man who invented it), now synonymous with theater surround sound and related technologies.

DOWNTIME - When the studio equipment (or person who runs it) is not working.

ECHO - Hearing a vocal or instrument a short period of time after the actual sound. Echo is also slang for reverb (reverberation), which simulates the sound of performing in a room or hall.

EQUALIZER - A device which alters tone, similar to the treble and bass controls on your stereo. Equalizers are usually more precise and can have up to 31 separate tone controls that allow the lowest to highest frequencies to be adjusted independently.

FADE - The reduction of volume of a sound source or the entire mix. Also called Fade-Out.

FADER - Mechanical device on a mixing console which accomplishes a fade. Usually a linear sliding device with a rectangular indented knob for easy finger placement.

FILTER - Electronic circuit that alters the sound of something by adding or removing a tonal component. Filters can be used to reduce rumble or hum, or reduce high-frequency hiss. The "wah-wah" pedal was in essence a variable filter under the control of one's foot.

GOBO - A dividing panel with sound absorbing material on both sides and sometimes a see-through panel. Used to help isolate singers or instruments when recording simultaneously in the same room (not in a booth).

HARMONIZER - Name of a digital device by Eventide Electronics that alters the pitch of sounds fed through it. Can be used to fatten vocals by doubling, or to add harmonies to a recorded sound. Raising or lowering the pitch too far results in artificial sounding vocals.

ISOLATION - The separation of sound sources acoustically so as to be more in control of them when mixing. Older recordings were done with less isolation than today.

ISOLATION BOOTH - An acoustically separated booth, usually for one or two singers, horns, loud guitar amplifiers, etc.

LEAKAGE - Sound from another source leaking into the microphone of another instrument or vocalist. Once recorded, it is difficult to remove without drastically affecting the intended sound.

LEVEL - Amount of audio signal (volume) on a recorded track. It is indicated by a meter on the tape deck or hard disk recorder.

LIMITING - Using a device (compressor/limiter) to keep the maximum level of sound from exceeding the recorder's limits. This helps to make vocals more intelligible by raising the average level of the performance (more severe than compression).

MIXDOWN SESSION - The time allotted to mixing all of the finished tracks down to a stereo master. Depending on the complexity of the session, this step can take a while to get right.

MULTITRACK RECORDER - A device which uses tape or computer disk to store individual sounds each on their own track. A 24-track deck can record 24 separate sounds or sound groups (more than one sound per track) on 24 tracks.

NOISE GATE - A device for removing noise between sounds such as breathing, headphone leakage, etc. This can be applied after recording so as not to eliminate anything during the performance. It is called a gate because it opens and closes much like a gate to let sounds pass.

ON-THE-FLY - Doing something in the studio while recording or mixing is taking place. An example would be manually adding delay (timed echoes) on certain words during a mixdown.

OPEN TRACK - A recording track that is empty and available for use.

OUTBOARD GEAR - Devices, usually mounted in racks (rack-mount gear) used for processing audio. Reverb, delay, pitch changer and compressor are types of outboard gear.

OUT TAKE - A recorded take that is not good enough to be used in the final product.

OVERDUBBING - Recording new tracks while listening to prerecorded tracks in synchronization ("in sync").

PATCH BAY - Switchboard-like collection of sockets where sounds can be routed to different parts of the studio and its equipment. Generally used for patching to outboard gear.

PATCH CORD - Special short cables used to connect sockets together on the patch bay to accomplish the above.

PUNCH-IN/OUT - Punch-in means to record over a section of a previously recorded tape track that one is trying to fix. This is done because a word or phrase or instrument part is not correct or not as good as one would like. Punching-out is the action of stopping the recording process after punching-in, thereby preserving the track from that point forward. This technique is done by the engineer on-the-fly.

ROUGH MIX - A quick mix not intended as the final mix. Usually done to make a tape for singers to practice with.

SCRATCH VOCAL - Rough vocal take not intended to be the finished one.

SLATING - Marking the beginning of a take or mix with a verbal identifying statement such as "Rock & Roll, take 1."

SMPTE TIME CODE - Society of Motion Picture and Television Engineers timing standard which places digital synchronizing code on a track of video or audio tape. This allows playback of video and audio together in sync. It also allows two or more multitrack recorders to run in sync, allowing for more tracks.

SOLO MODE - A button the engineer presses on the mixing console which isolates just that track for listening. More than one solo button can be pressed at a time.

SWEETENING - The process of adding music, voice and/or effects to an existing multitrack tape or videotape.

TALKBACK SYSTEM - The method by which the engineer can talk to the singer. This is accomplished by the engineer pressing the talkback button or by having a dedicated microphone channel "open" on the console.

TAKE - A recorded performance on one or more tracks.

VARISPEED (VSO) - Also called VARIABLE PITCH, this is the capability of changing the speed of the tape faster or slower by a small amount. This can be used to help match the tuning of an acoustic piano to other instruments after other tracks have been recorded, or to allow a singer to reach high notes that are difficult by slowing down the tape, thereby lowering the pitch. When the latter technique is used, however, the voice tone, when played back at normal speed, will sound different than if no varispeed was used at all.

VOLUME UNIT (VU) METER - The visual indicators that let the engineer keep the levels below the point where distortion can occur in the equipment. Most studio equipment has at least one visual meter per device to help keep distortion to a minimum and to maintain clarity and integrity of the sounds.

EXERCISES

1. If you have no studio experience, apply the steps in this chapter to become familiar with hearing your voice recorded for the first time.

2. If you are headed for the studio in your singing career, begin to research producers, using the information contained in this chapter.

CHAPTER 8

THE FINISHING TOUCHES

CREATING AN IMAGE FOR YOURSELF

Perhaps you've noticed that every successful artist has some kind of unique look or style that characterizes their image. Think of Madonna, Michael, Prince, Luther Vandross, Bruce Springsteen, Barbara Streisand, Tony Bennett, Brandy—the list goes on and on. From their hair to their make-up to their clothes and shoes, it's a well-orchestrated look. If you're fortunate enough to get an excellent record contract, the record company will include in your promotion budget money to hire a stylist. A stylist is someone who helps you coordinate your wardrobe, hair, accessories, etc. to create a unique style or look. Or sometimes your production company or manager will arrange for the stylist. Bear in mind, however, that all the money spent on the stylist's services must be paid back out of your royalties.

But what if you don't have someone to foot the bill for you and you don't have the money to hire a stylist yourself? Here are some ideas.

If you have a friend who is a designer or has a very good fashion sense, perhaps he or she will help you put a look together. But if you don't know anyone like this, you can do it yourself. Look at fashion magazines. Watch how the artists in videos are dressing. Go out to your favorite stores and try on clothes that are different from those others are wearing. Don't be afraid to try something entirely new for you. Your look can also be completely different than the way you dress when you aren't performing. For example, the members of the band Kiss would be unrecognizable on the street without their makeup and costumes.

Weight Considerations

Make sure the clothes you choose are flattering to your physique. If you're an overweight female, choose an outfit that doesn't emphasize your size. The entertainment business is cruel, and unfortunately, heavy women have a more difficult time trying to get a deal. Although some have become very successful, their number is small in comparison to successful slim ladies. However, in the worlds of classical, gospel, blues and jazz singing, not as much emphasis is placed on appearance. And even less importance is placed on the appearance of background and session singers, who are usually not in the spotlight. Female stars usually don't want a female back-up singer onstage who looks better that she does. And singers who do studio work exclusively can look and dress almost any way they want.

I recall being at a seminar for singers when a group of six women were called onstage to perform. They were introduced as the number one female session group in the industry—they were in numerous commercials and had sung many movie scores. You name it, they were doing it. But they were the most diverse mixture of women I had ever seen and were of all shapes, sizes and degrees of attractiveness. They were also from many different ethnic backgrounds. But when they started singing, their music was incredibly beautiful. They had every vocal category covered from soprano to bass, and I mean BASS—one of them had the lowest voice I have ever heard in a woman and could sing any notes required by a man's voice! Well, after they performed, they received two encores and got a standing ovation—they were *that* good! Because they didn't have the image the industry wanted to sell, they did session work.

In some cases, if you're not considered to fit into the typical industry mold, you can still use your unique appearance to your advantage. You just have to be *better* than the average singer. But my advice is if you're overweight or could just stand to lose a few pounds, lose the weight! If you have the opposite problem and are too thin, find clothes that flatter your body and show off your good features, then get yourself to a gym and build your body up to a size that is comfortable for you and pleasing to the audience.

It's hard enough as it is to break into the music industry—if you are overweight or underweight, don't make it even harder for yourself when it is possible to eliminate these problems with hard work and dedication. It's another part of being a professional and taking responsibility for yourself and your career.

Teeth

If you have defects in your teeth, get them fixed. There's nothing worse than watching a person sing who has missing, dirty, crooked or chipped teeth. If your breath is bad, then you probably need your teeth cleaned, or you may have other dental problems that need to be handled. Take care of your teeth and gums, because if you don't, you will lose them. And losing teeth will affect your singing!

Hair

Get a really good hair stylist to style your hair. A cheap "Super Dupercuts" job will not do! You're going to spend a little more money, but you're going to look a whole lot better. And you won't look like everyone else either. And if you really want to spice things up a bit, experiment with hair coloring. There are a lot of things you can do that don't have to be too dramatic, such as highlighting.

Hands

Both men and women should keep their hands clean and looking nice. Get a manicure. If you can't afford to have a professional one, give yourself one or get a friend to do it for you

Overall Appearance

One final thing! Always, always look clean and sharp when you're going out to appear anywhere, including when you go networking. (And that means lint free, with no unkempt wrinkles.) Your appearance is your presentation of yourself. Even if your style is that of a disheveled rock and roller or you have the grunge look, make sure you are clean and don't have body odor or bad breath.

Summary

If you will take the time to follow the suggestions in this chapter to put together an appropriate and attractive image for yourself, you will be putting the finishing touches on the product you are "selling"—yourself!

EXERCISES

1. Take a realistic look at your physical appearance and see if you need to lose or gain weight. Start an exercise program if you haven't already done so.

2. Research an image for yourself and begin putting it together with clothing and appropriate accessories.

3. Get your teeth fixed if they need it. Get your hair styled and your nails done if they need attention.

CHAPTER 9

THE BUSINESS SIDE OF THE BUSINESS

WAYS TO MAKE MONEY AS A VOCALIST

Let's go over some different ways you can earn a living as a singer. Here is a list of various types of singing jobs available.

1. Recording artist

2. Sessions singer

3. Jingle singer

4. Background singer for live acts

5. Musical theater performer

6. Voice teacher

7. Lounge singer in clubs

8. Soloist in churches

9. Opera

10. Casual singer (one who performs at weddings, bar mitzvahs, etc.)

11. Karaoke Jockey

12. Karaoke Singer (Contests)

Some of these jobs, such as sessions/commercials singer and background vocalist, overlap. However, some singers only do studio and session work and never perform live concert dates.

One thing you must know is that the competition to become a top notch session/jingle singer who makes lots of money is very stiff. You have to have a good ear, duplicate fast and more often than not be a good reader. You absolutely cannot sing out of tune! Also, you have to be able to work well with other singers. So succeeding at this can be easy or difficult—it depends on you. If you are professional and do your work, then you won't have any problems. If you do anything less than that, then you won't last very long in the sessions singing business.

If you want to be a back-up singer for famous live acts, you have to get into the clique that knows when the auditions are taking place. It's a very odd thing, but there is no formal clearinghouse for announcements of who's auditioning background singers for a tour. You have to know the right people, because the information is passed on by word of mouth. You'll hear about some jobs by joining AFTRA (a union for singers called the American Federation of Television and Radio Artists). At the AFTRA auditions be sure to network and get to know other artists—they often know about these types of auditions. Also, if you become a member of Singers United for Service , a support group for singers based in Los Angeles, you can network with other singers (tel/fax 213-386-5278).

To sing in musical theater, to be a soloist in church, or to do lounge singing, it's best to have a variety artist agent. (Any good bookstore with a comprehensive entertainment section should have books listing agents.) There are agents for casuals, usually called "specialty agents." Otherwise you have to know someone to get the bookings. However, as you do more jobs, your reputation will also spread by word of mouth and references. Usually casuals consist of weddings, bar mitzvahs, and parties. You usually work on weekends and can make good money. It's possible you could do two or three casuals a day and make $600.00 total if the party pays well. On this type of gig you have to know a lot of songs in many styles, from hiphop to jazz to standards. You also need to know some country, pop and soft rock.

To break into any of these areas, you have to have a demo. For jingle singing, you have to have a demo of yourself singing jingles. I know the next question: How do I get a demo of myself doing jingles when I've never recorded one? The answer is you have to make one. The best way to do that is to locate a producer who wants to produce some jingles to submit to commercial production companies so *he* can be hired to produce jingles for that company. However, AFTRA will not refer you to a producer to record his demos unless it's a union gig. You should look in industry magazines for that and get a referral. All legitimate commercials are done through the union and you are paid a very good session fee. More information on AFTRA is provided at the end of this chapter. Once you have a demo, you can go to AFTRA to get a list of the production companies that produce jingles and start sending the demo out.

There are also various singing jobs you can create yourself. Examples of such jobs include performing in the various promenades or doing singing telegrams.

These types of gigs pay money and get your chops really sharpened—you get a lot of practice and in some cases recognition. I've heard of people being discovered while singing on the street.

Going to karaoke rooms and entering the singing contests provides a good way for you to make money while getting practice performing in front of audiences. You can live off what you win while you are trying to get a record deal. For many singers, this is better than getting a straight job and they are improving their craft while they work. This may be easier for you to do if you live in one of the larger metropolitan areas with many clubs—singers I know simply travel around the greater Los Angeles and Orange County areas to the various karaoke clubs. But even if your geographical area has only a few karaoke clubs, you can still supplement your income a little by entering their contests.

You can also make a good living as a K.J.—Karaoke Jockey. But, as with anything else, you have to create your job. Some karaoke rooms are not full and others are, and the determining factor is the skill and charisma of the person running them.

By the way, if you decide that karaoke singing is as far as you want your singing career to go, that's fine, too! The information in this book can help you, no matter whether you decide to sing professionally full-time, as a sideline, or simply for enjoyment.

HOW TO GET INTO A BAND

There are several ways to get into a band. First, obviously, you have to find one. One way this is done is by word of mouth in the circuit. That means networking—going out to places where live bands perform. Talk to people who are already in bands and let people know you're a singer looking to get into a band. Tell them what kind of music you sing.

Check the various music trade magazines for bands looking for vocalists. Go to your local newsstand and ask for the trade papers that contain ads for singers. You can place an ad in a trade magazine, too. In Los Angeles and New York you can buy and advertise in *Music Connection*. There are also many other magazines that cater to actors and singers—*Dramalogue*, *The Hollywood Reporter*, and *Variety*. *The Hollywood Reporter* and *Variety* are the least likely to contain ads for singers for bands, but every now and then there is one. These are usually bands with management and possibly even a production deal or record deal pending. You should really have your act together if you intend to respond to one of these ads.

The first thing you will need is a demo tape to submit to the band leader or members. By the way, don't ever send out your only demo copy, thinking you're going to get it back. Those tapes are rarely, if ever, returned. It is also a good idea to put together a bio or resume of your experience as a vocalist. If you don't have much experience, then just write about yourself: where you're from, who you studied with, and anything else you can think of that would be a selling point for you.

Try to seek out a band that does the kind of music you really like to sing. Depending on the band's needs, you may be required to sing background vocals. If the band members are looking for a lead vocalist, then you'll need to ask a lot of questions to find out exactly what they are looking for. The more prepared you are, the better your chances are of being picked to be the lead vocalist.

For your interview, always look as good as you can in a way that matches the image of the band. After you submit your tape, you may be called to audition, but don't be discouraged if you don't get a response right away. When people are auditioning singers, they often have many tapes to go through and it can take a long time. But if you don't ever get a call-back, don't be discouraged! There can be many reasons why you were not called; it could be they already found what they were looking for, or they changed their mind about hiring a singer, or they went with a guy instead of a girl, or vice-versa.

If you do get the call and go to the next step, a live audition, always be professional and show up on time. If they want you to audition with one of their songs, see if you can pick up a copy and learn the song ahead of time. In addition to hearing you sing, they will want to see if they like you and you can get along with them, if you're dedicated, and so on. If everything clicks, then you'll be hired.

Here's something else to keep in mind. When Billy Sheehan was putting together his band, Mr. Big, he asked me to refer a singer for him. He told me that what was needed was 80% looks and the rest talent... wait a minute! Didn't that contradict almost everything I've said in this book about being good, professional, and having your basics in? Sure it did. But guess who actually got the job—Eric Martin. Have you ever heard Eric Martin sing? Not only does he look good, but he's an incredible singer!

BE CHOOSY WHO YOU WORK WITH

This is a good time to discuss the various types of musicians and bands that are out there. If you have your act together and have established yourself as a good singer, don't under any circumstances allow yourself to be surrounded by unprofessional musicians or singers. If you have one or more friends who need work on their craft or are not professional in their behavior, don't try to do them a favor by involving them in any of your projects. It will make you look bad and give you the reputation of being unprofessional. You can best help your friends by recommending that they take lessons and work hard to improve their skills—and read this book!

ALL-FEMALE GROUPS

This section is addressed particularly to female vocalists. What I have to tell you here may be a tough pill to swallow, but these are words that you would do well to heed if you hope to succeed in an all-girl group. And these cautions have nothing to do with an anti-feminist stance—having run my own voice school and production company for many years, I am very much in favor of women realizing their full potential.

It's a sad fact that most female vocal groups don't last, and joining an all-female singing group or band can be an invitation to trouble—even a nightmare. Statistically, more group failures occur with all-female groups than with guy groups. I've been in two girl groups and have known many female singers who have also been in them, and every single one ended in disaster. Nonetheless, I'm not really trying to discourage you from getting into a female group, but attempting to alert you of the statistics and suggest ways to avoid the problems and become successful—because on the positive side of the coin, if you can make it work, you stand to gain a lot. In recent years, all-female groups and female vocalists have been earning tremendous amounts of income for record labels.

What usually seems to happen is that egos get in the way of professionalism. Then things start to fall apart. The notable exception to this destructive pattern are groups in which the women are closely related. Examples of some of the famous ones are The Pointer Sisters, Sister Sledge, The Lennon Sisters, and The Andrews Sisters. All of these female groups are either still together or they sang together until they grew old and retired. A few of them ended when their members all quit the business together. My point is that these groups were and are dedicated to each other and stayed together and worked out whatever problems they had. They are more than family in name only—they are groups in the truest sense of the word.

Here's a sad-but-true story that illustrates the sort of thing that can happen if group members are unethical and don't stand up for what is right. I knew a girl group that had a ten-album deal with Arista Records with a nice hefty budget for each of the albums, along with an advance for each of the girls. One member of the group thought she was better than the rest and positioned herself as the group leader. She took advice from her boyfriend, who didn't know the first thing about the record business, and allowed their producer to call the shots without question. However, the producer was basically of criminal mentality and took most of the girls' advance money. He bought a house and put in a nice little recording studio for himself. The girl who had positioned herself as the leader was afraid of being thrown out of the group if she didn't go along with the producer's decisions. So she, of course, became the favorite of the producer and all but one of the girls in the group aligned themselves behind her. On top of all that, the producer's lawyer was representing the group *and* the producer, which was a conflict of interest.

The one independent-minded member who wanted to do the right thing tried to find a good manager for the group, but the producer disapproved every one of her choices. The rest of the girls went along with the producer's decisions because they were now also afraid of being replaced. The free thinker knew what the producer was doing and tried to get the other group members to see it. The producer then decided to get rid of the free thinker and, behind her back, auditioned other singers and found a replacement. He only told her about it after he'd hired the new singer to replace her.

The girls should have realized, before they hooked up with this producer, that in contrast with whatever negative things the producer told them to frighten them, they had their own value as a group. They had been in demand at several record companies. But instead they allowed themselves to be manipulated by an unscrupulous, conniving producer whose only goal was to further his career and line his pockets at their expense. The outcome was the producer's karma finally caught up with him. The entire project was shelved by Arista when the producer got too greedy and demanded more money to re-mix the album. Everybody lost.

What sorts of things should you watch out for to preserve peace and harmony in your group?

- Don't indulge in jealousy of other members. If you work hard, you will achieve your own success and fame.

- Don't go behind another group member's back to complain or say derogatory or untrue things about them to other members. Don't try to turn one member against another. Instead, have the courage and integrity to discuss your disagreements and needs openly and directly with that person.

- Don't fight about petty matters that don't make all that much difference in the grand scheme of things. Don't try to obtain a greater spotlight or advantage for yourself at the expense of other members. The audience loves a group that is together in voice and spirit; by the same token, they will sense disharmony in your group and be turned off by it.

Instead, and more than anything else, have a professional attitude and treat your singing group as a professional organization, just like any other kind of group you'd be a partner in. After all, it's a business no different than IBM—it's just a different product. This group is going to be your source of income for the next several years of your life. You need each other for the group to survive. If you have signed a contract and decided you are going to work together—if you are truly dedicated to each other—then treat your partnership as a business relationship and behave as a professional. Work out any disagreements or problems in a mature manner. Have a good sense of ethics, honesty and integrity. Be professional in how you handle and deal with the people in your band as well as the technicians who work for you. If you foster an attitude of mutual respect among all the members, you'll create a much easier working situation.

The advice in this section applies, of course, to both male and female groups. Females, however, need to pay special attention to these points.

WORKING WITH BAND MEMBERS

The vocalist or lead singer in a band is usually considered the front person, so your position as lead singer and front person will be a little difficult to hold if you're insecure about your voice. (The front person usually leads the group, announces the songs and does any other talking. The job can be shared if there's more than one singer.) Bands usually play loud and if your vocals are weak, some musicians will complain. So GET YOUR VOCALS TOGETHER!

Controlling the Volume of the Band

Many singers have problems hearing themselves while singing with a band. In most cases, it's the guitar and drums that are loudest for the singer. The drums are directly behind your head with cymbals crashing in your ears.

First make sure the volume problem isn't occurring because of a problem with the monitors—or your vocal technique! If your monitors are on the floor then you don't stand a chance of hearing yourself, because they won't be aimed high enough. You must have a good monitor system and it must be placed properly so you, the singer, can hear yourself. Your performance is fully as important as any of the other musicians in the group—or you wouldn't be there!

If your monitors are placed correctly and your vocals are strong but you still can't hear yourself, then, more often than not, the band is playing too loud. Unfortunately, musicians frequently have the attitude that the singer isn't any good if he or she can't sing over electronic amps turned up to ten and a drummer who is pounding on the drums as hard as he can. They seem to think that the singer can just scream... I mean *sing*, louder! The usual response from a musician being told to turn down is that if he does, he won't be able to hear himself play.

What do you do about it? Tell them to turn down! Or if you have a musical director, let him know the band is playing too loud so he can control their volume. If you *are* the leader/musical director of the band, you should get the entire band to turn down, get a good balance and listen to each other.

This can be a pretty tough thing to accomplish, because usually when the band starts to play again, the volume creeps back up as the band gets more and more into the music. For this reason you as the vocalist *must* earn the respect of the band so you can get them to do what you want.

Problems with Tempo

Another thing that can happen is the band may start playing a song too fast or too slow. Don't suffer through the song if you can get the drummer to speed up or slow down the time. This can be done very easily. Turn to the drummer and without making a big deal about it, let him or her know the pace of the song is not right, and give an indication of how it should be changed—slower or faster. You can do this without letting the audience know there is a problem. Then keep right on going like nothing happened and everything will be just fine. Don't stop the song and start over again unless there is an absolute disaster about to happen.

As an example of what superb audience control really means, I was watching a performance of the famous blues singer, Ray Charles, on national TV at a presidential inauguration. His band started his song too fast. He just shouted out to them, "Too fast, Too fast!" The band slowed down and no one in the audience seemed to mind.

The "Chick Singer" Vibe

As mentioned in Chapter 3, you can run into the "chick singer" vibe if you're a female vocalist in a mostly male band. That's when the guys in the band consider you to be "just a girl" and don't take anything you say very seriously. If you do complain, then you're being a "bitch."

As unjustified as such an attitude may be, reacting to it with hostility, complaining about it, or trying to "demand respect" without having earned it will just make things worse. The best way to avoid all these labels is simply to *be professional.* Do your job so well that the band members will *have* to listen to what you say. If you are well rehearsed, confident about your singing ability and have all your vocal tech in, you will be able to hold your position more easily under fire and you will earn the respect of the male band members. Good musicians don't want to work with a singer who sings out of tune and behaves unprofessionally.

When you have a legitimate complaint, make sure you get the band members' attention. Be *specific* with your complaint. If the band has a musical director, take the complaint to him. It's his job to make sure all the music is being played correctly.

As a living demonstration of these points, many female vocalists can be found in the business who have gained excellent reputations among musicians and are highly respected as professionals. And that's the goal of any singer among his or her peers.

Relationships Between Band Members

Another set of barriers can come up for female singers in a mostly male band. More often than not, one of the band members will develop a sexual interest in the female singer. Or the female vocalist will become interested in one of the band members. I've seen this happen even in bands where the singer was married to one of the band members. In one situation, the vocalist cheated on her husband with one of the band members. Even if it's a successful band with a very bright future, this kind of activity will break it up faster than anything else, and I don't recommend it. Only someone with very low self-esteem and no sense of ethics and integrity would intentionally go after someone who is married or already in a relationship with someone.

However, I'm not saying *never* get involved with another band member, because that doesn't work either. If you truly have a strong interest in someone in the band (who is unattached), no amount of denial is going to help you. But if you do start a relationship, keep things on a strictly professional level while working—keep it out of the band business. You have to learn to separate the two.

I am married to my keyboard player. We've been together for a long time and have a very solid relationship. We work very hard to keep the two parts of our lives separate. We NEVER bring any of our family problems into our rehearsals or performances. It's something that we, as professionals, are able to do. And the band members we work with are very respectful of us and our relationship. Neither one of us would even consider working with someone who didn't maintain this attitude. It would disrupt the vibe in the band and eventually cause problems that quite simply aren't worth the trouble.

Everything said, maintaining a professional attitude, making sure your vocal tech is good, and becoming trained musically will help you avoid all the above problems: not only will your increased musical awareness allow you to recognize and handle such difficulties rapidly and with no fuss, but your overall musical competence will earn you the respect of your fellow band members and increase your ability to play together as a very tight group.

GETTING A MANAGER

When Should I Get A Manager?

I've had consultations with many singers who come into my studio and think the first thing they need to do is to get themselves a manager. Yet most of them haven't developed their singing style, don't have a demo and have no idea what direction they are headed in musically. There are very few good, honest managers who are willing to take on a brand new singer who hasn't the slightest idea where she is headed. Why? Because a manager has to have something to manage. That means that you and your singing must be developed and good enough that people will be willing to pay to come hear you and buy your records. In other words, you must have a valuable product (your singing) that can be exchanged for money. When you have achieved this level of quality, the manager will be able do his job.

Now, there are some managers who will take on a new artist who is very young—say fifteen, sixteen or seventeen—and do what is known as grooming. They will totally create the image for the artist, pick the songs, pick the producers, find the record deal, and literally control and guide the entire future of the artist. In some cases they will invest a lot of money in the artist too. However, never for one instant think that all of that doesn't come without the artist giving up something. What you give up is money—sometimes a large percentage (as much as 25%)—and control of your future. Such a manager usually wants a percentage of *everything* you do that deals with the entertainment business. If you write a book, have a doll made in your image, endorse a product, or star in a movie and get paid for it, the manager gets part of it.

There's nothing wrong with a good manager getting a percentage of all your earnings, as long as he really was instrumental in helping you achieve your success. But keep in mind that you will also have to pay a percentage to your agent (if you act or do commercials) and your attorney (and sometimes two), who will negotiate your record contract for you. If you pay the attorney a flat fee instead of a percentage, you'll still probably pay more because you'll need the attorney to negotiate every contract you are sent. For example, if you write songs, you'll have a publishing contract as well as a contract for every movie and commercial you do. If you sing on someone's album, you'll have a contract.

So you see, getting a manager before you are ready can be a very costly affair. That's why there are so many horror stories around about how artists were ripped off by their managers or got stuck in a bad contract and now don't know how to get out. Getting a manager is a very serious career move and should not be done hastily or lightly.

In Chapter 10 of this book, "Interviews," Ken Kragen, the well-known and respected personal manager and producer, gives some excellent advice on seeking a manager. I strongly recommend that you thoroughly go over his interview as well as buy his book, *Life Is a Contact Sport: Ten Great Career Strategies That Work*. This book has helped me tremendously in my career.

Inform Yourself About the Business.

Before looking for a manager or a record deal, I strongly suggest that you get some books on the music industry and inform yourself about it as much as possible. The music industry can be a very tough, demanding, confusing and sometimes intimidating environment to work in, and you need to be armed with as much knowledge as you can get. I recommend *This Business of Music* by Sidney Shemel and M. William Krasilovsky. They have written several editions—get them all! Also attend seminars about the music business given by people you know have been successful in the business or are currently working in it.

Another eye-opening book is called *Hit Men: Power Brokers and Fast Money inside the Music Business*, by Frederick Dannen. It's all about the shady side of the business—who was and is involved, and the payola (favors given in exchange for getting records played). Because of the big payola scandals and arrests in past decades, business may appear to be conducted in a very above-board and legal manner these days. But if you don't think that "favors" and the concept of "greasing somebody's hand" still exist in the music business, you'd better think again. I'm telling you about this side of the business not to scare you off, but because you need to know that it exists. If you aren't aware of how some people play the game, you can become a victim. The music business is a very exciting and worthwhile activity, and for every shady businessman there are ten good guys. But as an artist you have to be aware of who you are dealing with so you aren't taken advantage of and don't find yourself unwittingly placed in an undesirable position. Examples of the types of situations that can cause problems appear throughout this chapter.

What Does a Good Manager Do?

What is the manager's job? A good manager is there to make sure you achieve *your* specific goals for yourself as an artist. The manager handles all business transactions and arrangements so you can devote all your attention and energies toward being an artist. The manager also serves as a buffer between you and the record company or anyone else you need to interact with on a business level. He will deal with the record company for you, handle any problems that arise, and let you know what is taking place.

How Can I Find a Good Manager?

So how do you find a good manager when you're ready? Sometimes you find one through references. You can get a directory containing the names of management companies and send them promo packages on you. However, most really top management firms don't take unsolicited material from unknown artists.

The best way to get a really good manager is to become really good at what you are doing artistically and start a buzz in the industry about yourself. Managers will soon be knocking on your door asking you to sign with them!

Management Contracts

One thing to keep in mind is that *no two contracts are ever the same.* If a manager gives you what he calls a "standard management" contract to sign, *take it directly to a lawyer.* Make sure you understand *everything* that contract says—if there is a *single word* in it you don't understand, *don't sign it!* You have the right to change things and to add things that you want to a contract. For example, you can have something called "exclusions" in your contract, which means you don't give the manager certain parts of your earnings, such as your acting income.

If you are given a contract to sign and the manager says you don't need to take it to a lawyer, RUN! If the manager gets upset because you want to take it to a lawyer, RUN FASTER! A good manager will allow you to read the contract and should advise you to take it to a lawyer before you sign it.

GETTING A RECORD DEAL

How Do I Get a Record Deal?

Everyone has a different story about how they got a record deal. You could say there is no set way of getting a deal. Some of the deals I discuss later in the chapter were accomplished with hard work, and some with luck. However, there *are* some basic and important things you need to do to prepare for your break and pave the way for getting a deal. So let's get on with a workable, practical plan that you can start on and use to actually make progress toward getting a record deal:

1. Have a very clear concept or idea of the kind of music you want to sing.

2. Make a very good demo, singing the kind of songs that really show off your vocal ability and that really excite the listener.

3. Make several copies and be sure to keep your master to make more copies with when you run out.

4. Put a package together that includes your demo, a short bio, and a photo. If you have any positive press clippings of you or your band, include copies of them, too.

5. Make sure the people you are going to shop your package to are legit. Remember, most record companies don't accept unsolicited material. So you will probably be giving your package to a manager, lawyer or producer first so they can shop it for you.

6. Book some shows where you can be seen by people and develop a following. Start a mailing list so you can let your public know where you will be performing. When you start to get a bite from the labels, they will want to see you perform live. Do yourself a favor and be prepared for it by doing as many shows as you can beforehand to get your show tight. You'll look really good if you have a lot of people at your show when you perform. Don't be discouraged if the label says they'll be there and they don't show up. I can't tell you the number of times that happened to us. One day, however, they actually did show up—and that's when we got a deal offer.

7. Most of all, BE PERSISTENT!

Now let's talk about these things in more detail. What follows is not what you ordinarily learn from a voice teacher—usually you just have to hit the street and learn from experience.

Be prepared to work hard and be really dedicated to your craft, because, as I mention above, the music industry can be a very tough and sometimes intimidating environment. You have to be willing to confront a lot of things—some good and some bad.

For example, there was a time when women singers were usually hit on for sexual favors in exchange for a deal. Have things improved? It's hard to say—now even men are hit on frequently. If you keep in mind what I said earlier in the book about how to handle business and sex, you're less likely to have problems in this area. Some of the offers are pretty tempting and extravagant. Some are even cleverly planned. I had a student who was having trouble getting her advance after she was signed. She found out one of the record company execs was jealous of her boyfriend and wanted her to break up with him before he would pay her advance. She told her manager what was going on and he promptly handled it.

After you've selected the songs you want to record by playing out (performing) and seeing which songs are the strongest based on audience reaction, it's time to go into the studio and do a demo of them. You should do a minimum of three songs. It's not necessary to do the entire CD. But you should do enough material so whoever you shop it to will get a clear idea of who you are, musically. Never, ever record songs in different styles, hoping to show your versatility. That will surely get you passed over because it'll look like you're unsure about your direction and indecisive about your music. They key word here is *focus*.

If you're fortunate enough to have the money to record an entire album—about ten to fifteen songs for a CD—then you can shop for what's called a production deal, or even start your own small independent label. You stand to make considerably more money this way than if you're signed with a major label, and you have more control over your product and your artistic creativity because, after all, you are your own boss.

If you decide, as a solo artist, to shop your record to a major label, or even to try to get a production deal, you need someone to shop it for you. That's when you need a good manager or an entertainment lawyer who knows the industry. These people can shop your CD to the correct A&R people at the various labels. By the way, "A&R" stands for Artists and Repertoire. For example, if your record is country, it shouldn't be given to the head of A&R for hip-hop or rap. If you already have a contact with an A&R rep at a label, but he or she is the rep for a different style of music, have that rep tell you who the A&R rep is for your style of music so you can get it to that person.

When you start to shop your record and you get a couple of rejections, try to find out why you were passed over. Sometimes this feedback can very helpful in getting your project fine-tuned. Other times you may get feedback that is too general, that you can't use to improve your songs. So only take those comments to heart that give you some idea of what may be missing for the listener. Remember, you have to convince the record company execs that they should sign you so you can sell records for them. If they don't think they can sell what you have, they will pass on you. So find out what about the music didn't communicate to the listener.

However, if the same songs communicated to your live audience big time, then perhaps the songs aren't really coming across in the recording. One possibility is that the recording doesn't meet the standard of quality the listener is accustomed to—so always make sure you have a professional demo.

The opposite applies too—if you sound great on tape, you may sell records (which is good). But if you then play live and sound bad, the negative word-of-mouth will eventually kill you.

A record company might also reject you if they don't like something or if they don't know how to categorize you so they can market you. But bear in mind that if the kind of feedback you're getting is telling you to go in a direction you don't really like or believe in, you might be shopping to the wrong A&R people. That's why you have to really know who you are and where you fit musically.

Remember when I said you have to be very persistent and be willing to be rejected a few times? When you're shot down, get up, knock off the dirt and keep right on going. You have to believe in your product, because if you don't, no one else will either.

Tips on Making the Record Deal

Keep in mind the proverb, "all that glitters is not gold," when you are offered a deal. Always, always read and make sure you understand everything in your contract. Yes, I have said this before—but I'm saying it again because it's so important. If at any point after you sign your deal, you find something wrong and are tempted to say, "I didn't know that's what that meant!" then you only have yourself to blame, because you didn't get your contract thoroughly explained to you. No one can trick you if you have your business together.

It is very important to be aware of the distribution provisions when negotiating your deal. "Distribution" refers to the placement of your records in stores in various markets or metropolitan areas throughout the country. Sometimes an artist's album is released and then the artist finds out that the distribution is poor. If good distribution isn't locked in when the deal is first struck, you can be asking for trouble: if you don't have a good distribution agreement, your record won't be available to be bought. What good is your CD being played on the radio if no one can find it in the stores to buy it? When radio stations find out that the record isn't in the stores, they won't play it.

Promotion money is needed for promoting the CD on radio and in magazines and to enable you to tour various markets to let people know it is on sale. When you hear various artists interviewed on radio stations and talking about their new CD's, realize that these interviews are frequently set up as part of a promotional campaign. When you strike a record deal, you also have to separately negotiate the amount that will be allocated for promotion. Sometimes labels will spend as much as $250,000 or more, depending on the popularity of the artist, to promote a CD.

How Other Artists Got Record Deals

Here are some stories that tell how various artists I know got record deals.

Mint Condition, one of the groups I teach, told me the story of how they got signed. They were session players and they backed up many singers. Finally, they took a look at what these people they were backing up were doing and decided they could do it too. They each took a turn singing to see who had the best voice and decided Stokley should be the lead vocalist. Then they made a demo and took it to Jimmy Jam and Terry Lewis and played it for them. Jimmy and Terry wanted to see them live after hearing the demo. They did a showcase and then they were signed.

Kevon Edmonds of the group After 7 worked in the pharmaceutical industry. His brother, producer Kenny (Babyface) Edmonds, told him he wanted to put him in a group with his other brother, Melvin, and a close friend, and record them. That's how they got their deal. See Kevon Edmonds' interview in Chapter 10 for the full story.

Luther Vandross was a session singer who sang back-up for a lot of big name acts. Eventually he started a group of his own and later got a deal as a solo artist.

A couple of other students of mine auditioned for a producer who was putting a group together for a production company. The singers were signed to the production company and the production company signed a deal with a label.

I also heard a story about an all-girl group that saw a well-known producer coming out of a building in New York. They approached him and told him they were singers and wanted to audition for him because they wanted a record deal. He said, "Okay, sing for me!" They said, "Right here on the street?" He said, "Yes." They did and blew him away—and he gave them a deal.

Another singer got a deal singing in karaoke bars.

One of my students recently got a deal with a referral from me and my husband. We told a friend who is a multi-platinum songwriter about her. He asked for a demo, which we gave him. The demo was strong enough for him to take an interest and he asked when he could see her. We had her fly down from her home in the San Francisco Bay area and sing for him in his studio. He liked her voice, her look and her personality and told her he would work with her when she moved to Los Angeles. However, by the time she was able to arrange to move, the songwriter was already on another project. He had also cooled off on her because although her vocals were good, she still needed work. He told her to keep taking lessons and bring him some songs she liked—which was a nice way of saying he wasn't interested any more. But she didn't give up! She studied with me for three dedicated, hard-working months. We also met with three other people who, though legitimate and very interested in signing her, turned out to be dead ends. Six months went by and then the first songwriter was ready to work with my student. When he heard her again, he was blown away by her voice. He and his writing partner wrote a song tailored just for her, tested it on the market and got incredible feedback. She was signed to their own label and the outcome is that this singer is currently on her way to stardom!

See John Novello's interview in Chapter 10 for more detailed information on getting a record deal and succeeding in the business.

Now That You Have a Deal, What Happens?

When you sign with a record company, you are working for them—they are your boss and they make the final decisions on the first song to be released as well as the order of release of the rest of your songs. They decide what the single will be. You are only allowed to participate in these decisions after you have a proven track record like that of a superstar such as Michael Jackson.

If the negotiations went well and your lawyer was good and got you most of what you wanted, you should have a nice advance. (An advance is money you get in advance of the sale of your record or CD that you will have to pay back to the label out of the earnings from your album). Your advance pays your living expenses while you record your tracks. If you got a budget of $250,000 to record your album and a $25,000 advance to live on, you owe the label $275,000. They have invested $275,000 in you against your royalties, which is the money you are expected to make from the sale of your records. The $250,000 is to pay for studio time, musicians, meals while recording, tape, mastering, etc. In short, you are responsible for delivering to the label a completed master of songs they can now duplicate, promote and market to people for sale.

Once your record is made, you've got to have a good promoter working your record. If the promoter is not very good, then your record won't be played very much. The promoter's job is to get your record played by as many stations as possible—and not just *any* radio station, either. Certain key stations must play the record before some of the major stations will even budge on it. Sometimes independent promoters are hired to promote a record, either in addition to or instead of the record company's own promoters.

I'm sure you've heard stories about the days when payola was the standard way things got done in the music industry. Payola is when someone does a favor for someone so they will play a record. The favor can be in the form of money, drugs, sexual favors, gifts, and so on. That type of thing is supposed to be nonexistent in the industry now, but I will say one thing: *Who you know* in the business plays a big part in your getting a record deal and in the success of your record. Favors are still done and there are certain artists who get preferential treatment over others. Have you ever noticed how some artists' records are heard once or maybe twice every hour, and other artists' records are heard only once the entire day? The program directors of the radio stations are wooed by the promoters. Each promoter has a certain region of the country that he "works" to get program directors to add their record to play lists. It's sad to say, but promoters frequently use whatever means of persuasion they can—legal or illegal—to get the program directors to play their clients' music.

Program directors also read various music industry newspapers which circulate valuable information throughout the music industry about new releases and which records they should be on the lookout for or playing. Some of these insider newspapers or "pick sheets" are *Radio Programmer, Hard Sheet, FMQB (Friday Morning Quarterback), R&R (Radio & Record), The Mac Report, Hits, The Gavin Report ...* and on and on! There are different newspapers for each style of music: rock, alternative, R&B, etc.

Unethical Conduct

Once you get a deal, you need to stay alert because, unfortunately, many things can still occur to turn it into a disaster before the record is even released. A lot of these fall under the broad heading of unethical behavior.

Here are two examples of how unethical behavior destroyed projects after an entire album had been recorded for a major label.

In one case, the producer got greedy and wanted more money when he was told by the president of the label to re-mix the album. But the president told him he'd already given him a quarter of a million for the record and he wasn't getting any more. So the project was shelved—and the original deal had been for ten albums on a major label with a budget of $250,000.00 for each album! What happened? Instead of using the money on the album, the producer had pocketed most of it, and bought a new house and built his own recording studio with it. The whole deal went up in smoke.

Another deal fell through when the manager suddenly started to make unreasonable demands to the label and to the artist he was managing. This was only the tip of the iceberg. The artist found out that the contract the manager had negotiated for him with the label had some hidden clauses in it that would have ripped him off for most of his royalties and publishing. Needless to say, the artist got out of the contract and fired the manager.

Occasionally a record company will try to pull a fast one over on you. Something that has happened to some well known artists—even those with many successful albums to their name—is they've recorded a new album only to have the record company execs reject it and put the entire project on the shelf. Then, some years later, the label went ahead and released those songs under the heading of "lost" or "never-before-released" recordings, and made a killing on them.

The best way to avoid these type of headaches is to *really know* who you are involved with and make sure you understand everything in your contract before you sign it. If you have any doubts or questions about *anything*, ask questions and investigate until you are 100% certain whether you should or should not go ahead.

You should also be aware that invitations or persuasion to indulge in unethical or illegal activities such as procuring and using drugs and/or prostitutes can come from unexpected directions, and at any point in your career. For example, some unethical record company executives who accompany their groups on tour may use the groups' gigs as an excuse to engage in drugs, illicit sex and other vices. They will frequently try to get the artists to go along with it. But these are invitations to disaster and the eventual ruin of your career and reputation. You should be prepared for such situations and know how you would deal with them if they come up.

WHAT'S AFTRA?

AFTRA, which stands for American Federation of Television and Radio Artists, is the union that singers join. Here is a description of AFTRA, reprinted with their permission:

> AFTRA was founded in 1937 to protect the wages and working conditions of the radio talent. Today AFTRA's membership includes recording artists and other performers working in the radio, television and recording industries.
>
> AFTRA's contractual areas of jurisdiction include sound recordings, television and radio programs, television and radio commercials, and non-broadcast recorded material. AFTRA negotiates wages, working conditions, and benefits for performers in all these fields, and ensures that employers comply with the applicable AFTRA Agreement under which a performer is working.

> **Becoming an AFTRA Member:**

> A performer may join AFTRA's Los Angeles Local by completing an application for membership and paying the full initiation fee and dues in cash, cashier's check or money order (or Visa/MasterCard in person only). If a performer elects to join prior to securing a work commitment by an AFTRA signatory company, the performer must sign a rider acknowledging AFTRA's advice that there is no

work guarantee or automatic access to membership in the other 4-A unions (which include Actors Equity Association, American Guild of Variety Artists, and Screen Actors Guild, as well as AFTRA).

The initiation fee is $800.00. Dues are payable twice a year, on May 1st and November 1st, and are based on the performer's gross earnings under AFTRA's jurisdiction for the previous year.

If you would like more information on AFTRA or would like to join, please call (213) 461-8111 in the Los Angeles area. The number for the National Signatory Department is (212) 532-0800.

EXERCISES

1. Pick out the various ways you'd like to earn money as a singer.

2. Prepare the necessary tapes, bio/resume, etc. that you will need to shop around to get work.

3. If you are part of a group and have a conflict with a member of your group, set up a meeting with that member and work out your differences. Come to an agreement that is workable for all involved so the group can survive.

4. Take a realistic look at where you are in your career and evaluate whether you are ready to sign with a manager. If you are ready to hire a manager to work for you, interview several and ask for references.

5. If you already have management, make sure you have a good open and honest relationship with your manager. If there are problems and you want to change your management, you may need to seek legal advice.

6. If your goal is to get a record deal, prepare yourself to shop for it using the information in the section "Getting a Record Deal."

CHAPTER 10

INTERVIEWS

The interviews in this chapter will provide you with insight into the careers of some highly respected and successful individuals working in various capacities in the music business. I've selected a manager, a session singer, two singers who are members of well known vocal groups (one of whom also has a career as a solo artist), a singer/songwriter/producer turned record company owner, a composer/musician, and a recording studio technician/sound engineer. These are the types of people you will interface with throughout your career.

In the following pages, you will hear what these pros went through to achieve their successes, and what actions and attitudes they consider most important. Most of them offer specific advice and recommendations for both beginning and more advanced singers. There are few better ways to learn something than through the personal experience of professionals who have already succeeded. Enjoy!

KEN KRAGEN

For over 30 years Ken Kragen has been involved in creating the most popular and innovative American shows and entertainment and guiding the careers of some of the most loved American entertainers. His credits read like a history of popular U.S. culture since the late 60's: He co-produced "The Smothers Brothers Comedy Hour" in the late 60's as well as their highly successful return to CBS television in the late 80's. Ken produced the famous Los Angeles stage musical *Hair* in 1968; he created the "Pat Paulson Campaign for President" TV Special in 1968; and he produced the musical *Lies & Legends (The Songs of Harry Chapin)* in 1982. Ken has also produced the three mini-series, four television movies and numerous musical specials starring Kenny Rogers from the late 70's all the way up to the present. In addition to his over 30 year representation of Kenny Rogers, Ken has managed many important entertainers including The Limeliters, Harry Chapin, The Smothers Brothers, Lionel Richie, Olivia-Newton John, Burt Reynolds, Trisha Yearwood and Travis Tritt.

But Ken's most notable achievements have perhaps been in the area of social and human betterment. Ken was the creator and organizer of the "We Are The World" African relief effort, both pulling together the 45 famous artists who performed the song and then creating the organization which supervised the raising and distribution of the funds. Subsequently desiring to heighten awareness and alleviate the problems of hunger and homelessness here in the United States, Ken developed the huge "Hands Across America" project, rallying some seven million Americans to stand hand-in-hand from the Atlantic to the Pacific. "Hands Across America" was the largest private fundraising effort ever carried out in America. Both efforts forever changed the country's awareness by bringing the issues of hunger and homelessness out of obscurity and focusing national media and public attention on them for the first time. For his work, Ken has won many civic awards as well as the highly coveted United Nations Peace Medal.

While continuing to represent clients and involve himself in various special projects, Ken teaches a course in personal management at the University of California at Los Angeles, is a sought-after speaker across the country, and consults with individuals and corporations at all levels. His book, *Life Is a Contact Sport: Ten Great Career Strategies That Work*, is "must" reading for anyone who would make their career dreams and goals a reality. In giving this interview, Ken was delighted to have the opportunity to help singers with career advice.

G: I notice that a lot of the artists you work with have some degree of experience in the industry or they know the ropes and know what to do. Most of the people that I work with are just beginning, and don't even know when they should start to look for a manager. So the first question I would like to ask is when should an artist or singer who is just starting out seek management?

K: Well this isn't the exactly the answer you're looking for, but it may work. What I tell anyone new is to find a really good entertainment attorney first, rather than a manager. It's hard to find a manager who you can trust. There aren't very many of them and almost every act gets burned early with management. A few of the acts survive. Managers come along who are kids the artists went to school with, or husbands and wives. A few of those develop into good managers. Narvel Blackstock is a good case in point; he's Reba McEntire's husband. So there are times that it really works out. But for every one of them that works there are perhaps 50 acts that got burned. So what I really tell people to do first is to find a reputable, decent entertainment lawyer. If they believe in you they'll work for very little to begin with. The good lawyers have a lot of contacts—they can find you a reputable manager and they can help you contact a record company and so on. That has always seemed to me to be the smartest route for somebody who is just starting out.

Another good thing is that a lawyer can help see that you get the right kind of agreement with a manager so that you don't get burned down the road. You know, I see these kids make it and then they have to extract themselves from really bad management deals. In other words, I don't think going to a manager is the first order of business.

An act should go to a lawyer who has good connections and the willingness to take you on. The First Edition came to me through a lawyer who persisted in staying after me. I get more recommendations for artists through lawyers. Trisha Yearwood came to me through a combination of the president of a record company and a lawyer. Her lawyer—who's still with her—is really first rate. Over the years the lawyers have most often been the ones to come to me and find me and also find record deals. So that's the best place to start.

G: OK.

K: Then, once you're looking for a manager—I think I may have said it in my book (*Life Is a Contact Sport*)—I have three or four criteria that I believe are the most important things. Above all else, find an honest person. Whether they have experience or not, whether they have the contacts or not, start with the fact that if they're not someone you can totally trust, you don't want them. No matter what else they've got.

G: Right.

K: You must have that kind of relationship, and you've got to check it out thoroughly. You've got to talk to people who have worked with the potential manager or dealt with them. Even if they don't have management experience, find out how they were to work with in past dealings. Be aware who this person is.

I think that the next thing is enthusiasm—their belief in you. Because with any new act—I don't care who it is—you have to bang down a lot of new doors and you've got to take a lot of rejection. In order to do that you've got to have that thorough belief in the artist's ability and be really willing to go through a lot for them. I think that is number two in the traits to look for.

The next thing to consider is how good is their judgment? Every manager has a different set of qualities. Some, like Peter Asher, were producers first. He was an artist and then he became a producer. This enabled him to manage his artists' careers while he produced their albums. Irv Azoff was a tough-driving negotiator—a really tough guy who worked really hard for his clients. Sandy Gallin is a manager who believes very strongly in his artists. He makes unbelievable deals for them because he approaches people thinking his clients are the biggest artists that ever happened. So when you try to negotiate with him, he's starting from a premise that this is the most important artist on the earth!

Everybody comes with totally different qualities and they are successful for different reasons. Management is not like any other area of the entertainment business because there is such an eclectic mix of people. There are all kinds of managers.

So first, you want honesty, and secondly you want enthusiasm and real belief in you, and then I think you start branching out into considering how good their judgment is. After that it's how much experience they have, what they have in the way of contacts, how good their knowledge is, and so on.

People who are honest and enthusiastic can pick up all the rest of it. I started out managing the Limeliters with absolutely no management experience. I made a lot of mistakes but I also helped the group become very successful.

G: Well that's the ultimate goal.

K: Yeah!

G: You suggested getting a lawyer. How would you recommend that a new singer or somebody who's just starting find a lawyer?

K: Ask a lot of people, read the trades, see who's representing who. It is probably a good idea to try to find a lawyer who represents artists in a similar category to your own, because that means they are probably dealing with record companies and other people in the industry who have similar interests. I'd pick out the ten acts that you most admire and find out who represents them. Find out if there is one lawyer who represents a lot of acts in that particular field. Start there.

G: What is the likelihood of a lawyer taking on a new client that's a developmental act?

K: Lawyers do it all the time.

G: More so then managers?

K: More so than any other group in our business. If there is legal work to be done, they can make money hourly or they'll take a percentage. Lawyers tend to be much broader in their willingness to take on new business. One lawyer, Owen Sloan, comes to me often with new talent that he's found and really believes in and is working hard for.

G: Are you still managing artists?

K: Oh yeah—I manage Kenny Rogers, Trisha Yearwood, Travis Tritt (with Gary Falcon), Ronn Lucas (with Michael Houbrick) and Linda Eder who is on Broadway now and is going to be a huge star.

G: I knew you were doing a lot of teaching and thought you might be so busy that you didn't have the time.

K: No, I'm doing a lot of different things. I have many projects. I'm producing a film about the life of Galileo. I'm working with the world's leading driver, drag racer John Force. Travis Tritt has become a certified driver. We did a TV special on drag racing and we are also developing a series for John Force.

G: What do you look for when you are about to take on a new artist to manage? Is there any special thing?

K: I look for somebody who is a decent, honest person. Most importantly perhaps, I want somebody who, in my judgment, has that extra quality, which is very hard to define, that says that this person can really be a star. And not a one-dimensional star, but somebody who can have some longevity—somebody I am truly excited about and believe in. And then I guess it's critical from my standpoint that I have some time—I need to be sure that I've got enough time to do a decent job for them. Usually the thing I have the least of is time.

G: Does the age of an artist make a difference to you?

K: I don't pay any attention to it. However, we are now in an era of younger and younger stars in many areas. For example, I'm at the drag races and there's a sixteen or seventeen-year-old girl who's racing against 50 year old men who have been racing all their lives, and she's winning. She grew up in it—her dad's wealthy and she grew up in the sport. She's the only one who can race in the teenage division and the pro division at the same time and she's doing very well. And you have it in tennis, and you have LeAnn Rimes with the top selling album in the world and Tiger Woods in golf, etc.

But I don't pay attention. In the first place, I'm not looking any more. I just get involved in situations where the people are totally unique, where there is something that excites me and I think the people are really special. When I think it's going to be fun. I don't think age is an issue at all. The lady I took on in New York is in her 30s, but she's just about to break as a new artist.

G: Was she recommended to you?

K: I became good friends with Frank Wildhorn, who has three shows on Broadway this year, and he said you've just got to hear my fiancée, she's really something. And when I heard her, it was just what he said, a cross between Barbra Streisand and Judy Garland. Sometimes she sounds so much like Streisand, you think it is her, but she can sing like Garland, she can belt, and with any luck she's going to take Broadway by storm. All the pieces were just sitting there—she had an album come out at the same time as the show's opening, and she's got a job on Broadway for the next year. So although I didn't have a lot of time, this was going to be fairly easy because she is sitting in a Broadway show.

G: What show is she in?

K: She's in a show called *Jekyll and Hyde*.

G: The title of your book, *Life Is a Contact Sport*, is really appropriate because many of your artists and projects seem to originate from meeting someone who then refers you to someone else—that's how this last one happened.

K: Things happen all the time if you're constantly open to the opportunities.

G: Would you say then that it's really vital that a person pays attention to who they are talking to?

K: Yes, and what's going on. On the other hand, I don't ever start by trying to exploit the situation. Things come much more naturally if you aren't always looking to make something out of every situation. I don't go into it that way, but I am always aware of who I'm sitting next to on the airplane—I talk to them. It's amazing—you keep your eyes open, you read the trades—you're just always looking. I find ideas for my clients everywhere. I'll open a newspaper and there's something that'll spark a thought; or I'll be in a conversation with somebody and something will come up.

I ran into Jay Coleman backstage in the audience at the Grammys a few years ago. He was looking for somebody for a Revlon deal. Two weeks later Trisha Yearwood had a deal with Revlon because Wynona had just turned it down. Things are always out there if you're really open to it. Opportunities are everywhere.

G: So you just have to be perceptive enough to recognize it. Now here's my final question—do you have any advice for a singer who wants a record deal?

K: Well, number one you've got to have a decent demo. It can't be a halfway one. It's got to be a good one. So for starters, you have to have something that showcases you—a video, a demo—you've got to have the tools with which to sell yourself. So you've got to find a way to invest in that. And it's become easier and easier nowadays, with synthesizers and the other options available, to get a decent product in demo form. But do something first class to begin with that shows you off properly, because that's going to impress somebody. That's the first thing.

Then I think it comes back to the same thing I said about managers: first I'd just go find a good lawyer who has a lot of contact with record companies in the area in which your vocal quality lies, or with companies that are recording the kind of music you are interested in. And then I'd really examine the marketplace. It's what I'm talking about in my book when I mention backwards thinking. Think about who the gatekeepers are and what they are looking for and what they are going to want. Talk to people to find those answers. Go in prepared, do your homework and don't be naive about it.

G: Everything you've said parallels the contents of your book, and I am recommending that my readers get it. Thanks for taking the time out of your busy schedule to do this interview.

KEVON EDMONDS

Kevon Edmonds is the originator and driving force behind the group After 7, known for their elegant vocal stylings tinged with a cool, 90's edge. After 7 is made up of brothers Kevon and Melvin Edmonds and Keith Mitchell. Onstage, they're reminiscent of 60's style all-male groups, but their music sets the scene and creates a contemporary presence that provides the best of both eras. After 7 is known as one of the premier vocal groups in pop and R&B music.

And Kevon is considered to be one of the finest male vocalists in the music industry today by his peers. Having had success come at a time in his musical career when most artists would consider themselves "too old," his views on the industry are full of insight and knowledge. His refreshing viewpoint of the image After 7 projects is exactly what's needed in today's music industry. Kevon says, "I want people to think of After 7 as positive male figures. Men who respect women. Men who have an appreciation for relationships and live songs. Now, we're not angels, but we basically try to do the right thing. We've grown up learning to try to stay on the right path."

Kevon is very proud of his successful younger brother, Kenneth "Babyface" Edmonds, who has produced and written material for After 7. Kevon is happy to have been blessed with the success he and his family have attained.

G: How long have you been a singer?

K: I've been a singer most of my life. I pretty much sang for my own enjoyment—it wasn't anything that I necessarily shared, because as a child I was pretty shy. I used to enjoy singing along with commercials and things like that. But I was really pretty bashful and was uneasy about getting up in front of people and singing out.

G: When did you decide you wanted to do it professionally?

K: I didn't really consider doing it professionally until I was about nineteen.

G: When you were in school did you study music, or anything like that?

K: Nothing. I never had any formal music training. But when I attended Indiana University I enrolled in a five hour credit course called the I.U. Soul Review. That class taught the practical application of singing and performing. So we learned a little bit about business, about music and putting ensembles together. There were two different rhythm sections that each learned a certain number of songs for each act, which included an all-male group or a mixed-gender group, and an all-female group. And we would take this show out on the road and perform before high schools and other colleges. That was really the first time that I got a taste of what performing involved, as well as doing the type of music that I grew up with.

G: What kind of music was that?

K: We basically did Top 40 and the most popular R&B songs.

G: But didn't you start in a group, as well?

K: Yes, when I was very, very young, thirteen or fourteen years old, we were in a group called Indy Five. It consisted of me, my brother Babyface, and two other guys. We did performances for various adult functions, but not anything that allowed us to perform in front of kids or anything like that. That, I guess, was my first actual taste of performing. It wasn't something that rushed to the forefront of my mind, like, "God, this is what I want to do!"

G: It was something to fool around with as a kid?

K: Exactly.

G: What you're telling me parallels with what Janis Siegel from Manhattan Transfer did. She started in a group of girls when she was twelve years old, and all they did was go around and sing for friends and family, for the fun of it.

K: Right—we didn't have a record deal and no one knew who we were. I think that initially it makes it difficult for anyone to buy into who you are—often the people who come out to support you are normal people who have come out to some function or activity to see you perform. They think, "Here are some nice kids singing for fun."

G: How long did it take you, from the time you were nineteen, to actually get into something solid?

K: The group After 7 was the first solid thing that my brother Melvin and I had the opportunity to participate in. I was about 31 or 32 when the door really opened. And it opened as a result of my brother Babyface and his writing partner, L.A., beginning to have some success. Business propositions were offered to them by record labels all the time, and Virgin Records, the label that we are still presently signed to, offered them a production deal and asked them to bring them three acts. We were their first choice. However, when the word came down that they were interested in us, the group had not actually been formed yet.

Keith, the third member of After 7, was a friend I had met down at Indiana University, and he had been in the male vocal group I sang in. From being in that group together, we found there was a common interest for both of us, and even in the summer months off we would get with my brother Melvin and do some harmonizing—just because the love was still there. We didn't really feel like "turning it off" when school was out. It must have been about 1978 when I left Indiana University. I wasn't exactly sure what it was I wanted, and I didn't feel like I was doing justice by being in school at the time.

G: What were you studying in school?

K: Well, I went for psychology. And somewhere along the line my interest changed to telecommunications. But then I started to get a real interest in music for the first time, and it opened up another door for me, in terms of what I really may have aspired to do. And being in the I.U. Soul Review kind of got me on another road. So my interest in pursuing telecommunications took a back seat—it wasn't as pressing to me as my love of music. And I was just really discovering that for the first time.

But I also wanted to understand a little more about the business side of the field I wanted to pursue. My intent was to learn as much as I could before actually getting into music. I had an opportunity to worked as an assistant manager for the group my brother was a member of, called Man Child. But, as luck would have it, their group was signed to a label called Chi Sound, a subsidiary label of United Artists Records. So when United Artists closed down their music division, of course that record company folded and so did the group's opportunity to continue to record. And I lost my assistant management job.

G: What happened then?

K: I had to determine where I would go from there, and there weren't any other management opportunities out there at the time. You know, life takes you on certain roads, and everybody has to do what they have to do—it doesn't stop the bills from coming in or anything like that. So I ended up getting a job—a job that I thought I would only work for maybe a year or two at the max. Three... five... seven...

G: Is that how long you worked the straight job?

K: I ended up being at that job nine and a half, nearly ten years. But during that time I never let go of what was becoming a dream, as far as music was concerned—music in some sort of fashion. While I was employed at that company, my brother Melvin and I would drive from Indianapolis to Cincinnati, where my brother Face was living. He and L.A. had joined a group called The Deele. And we would commute back and forth and do demo tapes on the weekends. My brother Kenny was submitting them to other groups he wanted to produce or to write for. We would be the voices on those tapes. But at the same time, it allowed us the opportunity to hone our skills. And as time went on, we began to try to put demos together so that we could submit them for our own opportunities.

We came really close at one point; I think it was Quest Records. But somewhere along the line there was a communication breakdown and it didn't happen. So you learn to take it on the chin—to pick yourself up and pull it together and get back to the flow of things.

And different times you have the dream. You shoot your shot and get knocked down a little bit and you come back up and you shoot your shot again. There were about three such attempts in that time period.

And there was a low period, where everybody just kind of purged it out of their system for a minute. But it began to kind of well up in us again. It welled up in me again and I knew that I was reaching a point where I had to make a decision with what I wanted to do in my life, because I wasn't happy. I was making a living—I was taking care of my financial obligations and so on, but I wasn't really happy with it, and I knew that I couldn't go on doing this for the next 25 or 30 years. I just didn't want that.

G: What was the job that you had?

K: I was working in production at a pharmaceutical company. I can't even remember what it was I was doing. But I just didn't feel like I wanted to do that any more. I knew I had to make a decision, and I reached out to my brother and said, "Look, you know, I don't care what it is. You let me know what needs to be done. I will do whatever needs to be done. I will carry your bags, A-B-C-D, whatever. But this just isn't going to work for me." And he said, "Okay, well just hold tight because we may have some opportunities that are unfolding for us as well."

And it was about a year and a half later he gave me a call in response to what we had talked about. We talked about who to consider for the group, and of course my brother, Melvin, would be a shoe-in. Then we talked about who else would be right and who we could audition. I remembered the guy I used to sing with down at Indiana University, Keith. We could have auditioned him, but I didn't choose to. I asked him if he still desired to do this, and he began bouncing off the walls when I told him about the opportunity. He was ready to go! He is now one of the members of After 7. So Face just told us to take the time, in the year to follow, to try to pay our bills and get our business in order as best we could. Be ready to make the transition when the opportunity comes. It was like a breath of fresh air for us.

G: You said earlier that the group had actually not been formed yet.

K: We hadn't been doing anything actively for several years, and even when we did do things, we would just get up and perform impromptu, if there was a band that knew a song. We'd sing, do gong shows and things of that nature. We didn't have a band.

G: Do talent shows?

K: Little talent shows. And "Star Search" type things. You know, you just try your hand in all of that stuff. But that was about as far as we took it, outside of whatever we did inside a makeshift studio. We never had an opportunity up to that point to go into a studio and work—we really didn't know what the inside of a studio was like. So when Face told us about the opportunity, it was like a shining light.

G: That's a good story because a lot of people will just give up after a certain amount of time. But you just persisted.

K: I was persistent, but then too, I had entree to an individual who at that time, though he was not a well known producer as he is today, was someone who was trying to carve his way. And he had some successes. He had produced Pebbles, and produced Whispers, and I think was getting ready to start working with The Boys ("Dial My Heart"). He was producing some of the other artists over at Solar Records, and was getting a handle on it.

So everyone was saying, "Well of course you could do it—your brother made it happen for you." And I can't deny that had he not reached out to us, it probably would have been very difficult, and probably continued to be very discouraging—Indianapolis doesn't offer a lot of outlets for someone to pursue music. Finding a connection somewhere in Indianapolis to open the doors to the music business just wasn't happening.

G: But the thing is, often when someone comes from a very famous family or has their foot in the door for some other reason, still, that person who is getting pulled in has to deliver.

K: Right. Well, we knew the burden was on us and we were going to come under fire for quite some time. I personally never minded it. I knew that ultimately, to stay around, we had to prove ourselves. But long before the opportunity availed itself to us, I was just plain proud of my younger brother. And I'm still proud of my brother's accomplishments, and if he opened the door for me, so what! Maybe now people have begun to accept the fact that the talent is real. I would have opened the door for him in the same fashion he did for us. So, it really didn't bother me.

G: Do you play any instruments?

K: No. But I think that I would just love to learn to play the piano—for myself, out of love—not to impress anyone. And if writing came from it that would be nice. I don't even want to use the word "master" an instrument, but just have an instrument that I could play. That would be a comfort for me, you know.

G: How many managers have you had?

K: As a professional act, After 7 has had four managers.

G: And you just kept changing until you got the right one?

K: Right.

G: And weren't you managing the group at one time?

K: Yes, we were self managing ourselves for awhile. But it just becomes a bit too tedious to cover all the bases that you need to cover as an artist. It's one thing to manage the road, be out there. That's not as difficult as being able to interface with a record label and be the act itself.

Record companies aren't generally receptive to dealing with artists who manage themselves—they don't want to take the meetings. They dodge you, they think you're going to blow up on them. And understandably so, because an artist typically is more emotional about their creativity and their art, and when somebody tries to strip them (take the creative control out of the artist's hands and enforce their own thinking on him or her) or direct things in a way that is not suitable to the creator of the music form, it's offensive. Sometimes tempers will fly and things get said that don't need to be said. An artist doesn't need to go in there and alienate himself from a record company who could possibly do him harm in the event they don't like what he has to say. They can get a chip on their shoulder, if they take it personally. It just creates a scenario for tenuous circumstances that you don't need to get yourself into.

You're best to leave yourself in a position of being loved by your record label. It's better to have a mouthpiece, someone to represent you within the walls of the record company, because the record company *has* to take a meeting with your manager and they have to hash out the differences with him because he represents your interests. They should be able to say to a manager whatever they want to say—and however they want to say it, too. That way they don't have to feel bad about having upset the artist, and the point is made.

G: That's very wise.

K: You learn.

G: Did you have a manager before you got your deal, or after you got your deal?

K: We had the deal before we had management. Our first manager came in when we were about a song away from completing. But we had done the bulk of the work prior to him coming to the situation.

G: So you had the direction of your group sorted out. A lot of singers say, "Well, I'm going to get a manager now, and then I'll get a deal."

K: But if you have the goods, sometimes it takes a manager to go in there and shop a deal, because some artists are so far removed from the people you need to know in order to go and get a deal. So sometimes managers are instrumental. But if you have connections and the product is good, by not having a manager you're eliminating an individual who is just going to come in there and take a commission on advances or something of that nature—you don't need that, if you can help it.

G: Any close calls with any crooks in the industry?

K: There are bad guys all over the place. And we've been "had"— it's part of growing in this business. Hopefully, it doesn't have to happen to everybody, but there seems to be a mindset in this business to some degree that "you got to go through it to get to it" and "you gotta get yours first." They say somebody's got to get you before you get to where you're going, and you've got to grease the palms along the way before everybody decides to let you alone. No need to name names. Trust me, they're out there.

G: Tell me about touring. Are your tours pretty smooth? Do you have a tour manager or do you manage yourself on tour?

K: No, we have a tour manager who basically sees to it that everything is taken care of. We have a tour manager, production manager, and a stage manager. It can get to be a pretty big entourage when you are out there sometimes, but it does make life a little bit easier. When we've been on the road, it's always been a pretty smooth operation. However, there are younger acts out here that sometimes get caught up in situations after concerts and all kinds of interfacing that is unnecessary. We have never been a group to get involved in any of that kind of stuff. We go. We're on time. We hit stage. We leave stage, and we roll out. And we move on to the next city. That is how we do it. We try to be as efficient as we possibly can. All of us are in our thirties or older. When we came into the situation, we had a more mature outlook and perspective on things. So it was about business, and we have always had the attitude that it is a business.

Actually, it's interesting, because while having been out here over these last seven years, some of the fans who we have gone and performed before time and time again over the years have said, "You guys seem a little different." It's because at first, even though we recognized that it was a business, it was all new and everybody was having fun with it too. But as you work in the business a little longer, you recognize the importance of what you are doing more than you did when you first got into it. Now you have the attitude, "Let's really be about business."

And I think that is what people recognize. They say, "You guys are so serious," and so on. Not that we can't have fun or can't have a good time, but we have learned that this truly is about being as efficient as you can and avoiding any unnecessary situations whenever you can. Sometimes going to a club afterward is just enough for something to go wrong. Our intent is start the tour, be on time, give one-hundred percent, be as professional as we can and complete the tour. There are a lot of acts that come out here and start a tour, that don't complete it for this or that reason—somebody got sick, somebody got hurt. We try to stay healthy. That's our focal point. We're out here to do a job, and we are out here because people are willing to pay, and that is what we recognize. When we hit the stage, we realize that we are there for the fans. They are not here for us.

G: What about drugs?

K: It's out there. Again, that is a situation that you have to avoid, because it's everywhere. And it doesn't necessarily walk up to you—there are situations where it's in the peripheral. Sometimes it comes from people in the business whom one would never expect to tempt you down the wrong path. It comes in so many different faces and shapes and forms that you have to have a mindset that it's not anything you want to be involved with. You almost have to send a signal—to have a buffer so that those people aren't able to get around you, get to you, or know where you're staying, because they will do whatever they can do just to get that party going. I think that we have been very, very fortunate. We could have fallen along the way. I thank God, you know; He's blessed us. He's kept us pretty strong. The temptation is always out there.

But it's a matter of where your head is, what your mindset is. What I know is that it's not going to do you any good, so it's better to stay away. It's part of staying healthy. And you know, you can't deliver your best with drugs. What is your focus? Your main concern while you're out there is to give a great show night after night. You can't do that with drugs, you know.

G: What do you do to warm up or prepare for a show? Do you sing scales or anything like that?

K: Actually what I do is eat! About two hours before the show I have to have a real good soul food meal. If I don't have that then I'm stressed and just not comfortable on stage. I also drink a cup of throat coat tea.

G: How do you make sure the type of food you like is going to be there for you? Is it a rider in your contract?

K: Yes. If the promoter can't find someone to prepare the kind of food I want, then I have someone find a good restaurant to prepare the food for me before the show.

G: How do you get along with your group members?

K: It's a high and low tide situation sometimes, so you have to try to find the medium. There have been times where it was really, really rough—initially it was. And I think it was because all of us were grown men used to doing things our own way. Everyone had their own places. Then, all of a sudden, you decide you want to do this and a sacrifice has to be made. And that includes giving up your privacy—everyone has to be crammed together all at once. You are forced to live in the same house, work in the same place, come home and retire in the same place. It was tough, because everybody was grown and nobody particularly cared to have to answer to anybody. But everything that you were before is neither here nor there. So it took a while for all of us to grow and to become adjusted to the fact that this was the deal that we made. I think that our desire to do this was strong enough to keep us together, as group members. I have a brother in the group as well, and of course, he and I went rounds. But you have your talks afterwards and you patch things up and apologies are made. You have to find different ways to get a breather.

G: Is Melvin younger than you too?

K: No, he's older. So we're different, but we're also alike in a lot of ways, and so I think that is where the resistance comes from. He may not back down from anything and I'm not going to back down from anything. So you get one of those little confrontations every now and again.

G: Did it ever come to blows?

K: No, no ones ever hit anybody. We may have wrestled or something like that. You know that after you let the steam out, you have to get back to business, and there are more important things than whatever the differences may be. They are minor and pale in comparison to our obligation not only to our fans, but to the fact that this is something we do to make a living. And we are blessed to be doing this. Those are the things that we always come back to and realize that whatever we're tripping about, we need to get over it and get back to business.

G: Do your disagreements ever involve the music—who gets what solo or things like that?

K: It's been very, very few times that we've disagreed about anything musical that I can recall. It's mostly been about trivial things.

G: Is there any advice you could give a singer trying to get into the business or trying to get a record deal?

K: Yes. First I would say that you have to love what you do. I mean really, really truly be in love with it, so that you can't do without it—something that you do day in, day out and could never find yourself away from because you are so much into it. It has to be the kind of love that you are willing to sacrifice a lot for. And making a sacrifice doesn't mean that success comes along just because you made the sacrifice. So that's how much you have to love the music or the singing, because this is an extremely tough business. For people on the outside looking in, it appears to be something very grand. But it is only very grand for a very minute percentage, a handful of people. But this is not meant to be discouraging, but to perhaps open people's eyes to what all of this is out here. Like I said, very few really make it and have the kind of success that people dream about.

It's a sad scenario, moreover, for a lot of black artists. The returns just aren't that great. If you choose to get into it, try to become as knowledgeable about it as you possibly can. It's good to master one thing and be very good at it, but it's not a bad idea to try to spread your talent. If you write or you produce, definitely try to hone your skills in those areas in addition to performing as an artist, because you don't want to find yourself pigeonholed and only able to do one thing. The reason is that there is no guarantee, as there is no guarantee in life about anything that we do. But also, the chances for an artist seem slimmer, because the people who tend to get paid in this business are the people who handle the business. The people who usually make the money are the record labels, the managers, the agents, the business accounts. Those people are the people who continue to generate income. The artists are usually the last ones to get paid. Even though you may be the focal point as the artist, you may still get the least amount out of the picture if you don't try to spread your talent. So if you can produce, write, or get into publishing, you should.

So if music is something that you really love, and it's a dream, stick with your dream, but know that reality is on the other side.

G: Very wise!

K: Tough business!

G: Thank you very much.

JANIS SIEGEL

Janis Siegel is a founding member of the internationally renowned jazz vocal group, The Manhattan Transfer. Janis and the group have won numerous awards including nine Grammys and fifteen Grammy nominations, the New York Music Award for Best Jazz Vocalist in 1990, the 1994 *Playboy* Magazine Critics Poll for Best Jazz Vocal Group and the *Downbeat* Magazine Poll for Best Jazz Vocal Group 1980-1990. Janis won a Grammy for Best Vocal Arrangement for "Birdland" and also holds an Honorary Doctor of Music from Berklee School of Music. Her second solo album, "At Home," which featured instrumentalists David Sanborn and Branford Marsalis, garnered her a Grammy nomination for Best Female Jazz Vocal.

Janis has recorded eighteen albums with The Manhattan Transfer and five solo album projects. She has performed with jazz greats Bobby McFerrin, Dianne Reeves and Jon Hendricks at the Playboy Jazz Festival and The Great American Music Hall in San Francisco and has appeared solo at the Monterey Jazz Festival and the Tri-C Jazz Festival. She has performed many times with The Manhattan Transfer on major television shows like "The Tonight Show," "Entertainment Tonight," "Good Morning America" and "Soul Train" as well as on variety specials all over the world. The group has also recorded soundtracks for major motion pictures such as *Dick Tracy*, *A League of Their Own*, *Swing Kids*, *Hudson Hawk*, and *Sharkey's Machine*. In addition, they have sung commercials for products such as Diet Coke, American Express and Sara Lee, among many others.

Janis continues her very active singing career, both solo and with The Manhattan Transfer. In recent years she has collaborated with pianist Fred Hersch, touring extensively in the U.S. and Japan and doing concerts, live radio performances and TV appearances. Their first album, "Short Stories," earned them a Grammy nomination.

G: How long have you been singing?

J: I have been singing professionally since I was twelve years old. So that would be 32 years.

G: How did you know that you wanted to become a professional singer?

J: I didn't really know until I was about seventeen, which is still pretty early. Singing was always something that I just did effortlessly, that I enjoyed doing, that was completely natural—singing harmony was always natural. I just did it. I didn't go to professional school or any of that stuff. I had a singing group, and we made records at a very early age. We were like freaks. We were twelve, thirteen year-old girls who played our own instruments and we made singles. At that time, you didn't get an album deal unless you sold a lot of records. You just got a singles deal.

G: What was the name of the group?

J: It was called The Young Generation. We were on Redbird Records, which had the Shangrilas, and Patti LaBelle and the Blue Bells. It was just something that we did, like other kids played baseball or took sewing classes—it's what we did in our spare time.

But I always thought, well, I am going to have to go to college and do something, have a career, be professional at something. And for some reason, music never occurred to me. Our parents, all three sets of parents, wanted us to be as normal as possible, and stay in school, you know.

G: You mean each of the girls in the group?

J: Yes, there were three girls, and we were all the same age.

G: Were you doing jazz then?

J: No, not at all. Pop mostly, and folk music. Stuff like Herman's Hermits' "Mrs. Brown, You've Got a Lovely Daughter," complete with ersatz English accents. We did "Do-Wah-Diddy," "The Cruel War's Raging," stuff with a lot of harmony—pop music of the time that we liked and folk songs like "Lemon Tree." We did our own vocal arrangements and we all learned the chords and we worked out little parts. We had outfits, even did a little choreography. I remember that we did some Beatles songs.

When I was in high school I started listening to jazz and it became a private passion of mine. What I was into was more like post-Bop-Coltrane, Pharaoh Sanders, and it had nothing to do with what I was singing. After high school I got a nursing scholarship to a school in Buffalo, New York. And after I got there, I realized that I couldn't relate to one person in my class—they were all so serious! I was really not that serious at the time—although I loved anatomy. I was more interested in playing music. I took a history of jazz course, with Archie Shepp, and I met a saxophone player at the school named Jay Beckenstein. He and I became very good friends and started to play and perform together up there. He would practice his scales all the time. He ended up staying in Buffalo, majoring in music, graduating, and starting a group called Spyro Gyra.

G: All this was while you were in nursing school.

J: Yes. And I left after a year. That's when I decided to be a singer.

G: Were you always singing when you were a kid?

J: I don't think unusually so. My father would always sing in the car, and he had a very nice voice—very much like Bing Crosby. He still does. He has a very relaxed, crooning style. He would get in the car and start singing, and I did too. I always used to sing harmony with him. That's really where I started. And then I was in chorus in school, which I really liked, but I never had an exceptional voice—I wasn't picked for the solos. I sang alto and soprano at that time. In high school I was in the yearly "Sing" show and did a few of those, but I wasn't anything extraordinary.

G: You weren't the stand-out singer?

J: No, no, not at all.

G: Did you have any stage fright when you were really young? Or did you just like singing?

J: I just liked singing. I remember singing for the first time in public when I was in second grade. I sang "Too-Ra-Loo-Ra-Loo-Ra" at assembly. That was at the suggestion of Mrs. O'Riorden, my second grade teacher. And that is my first memory of singing in public.

G: Where did you grow up?

J: In Brooklyn, New York.

G: Did your parents encourage you to sing?

J: I don't know if they really noticed that much. I was neither discouraged or nurtured. The big event in my life, though, was my favorite aunt buying me a guitar. She gave me a beautiful, acoustic Martin guitar and I taught myself how to play.

G: Was this when you had the group?

J: This was right before I had the group.

G: So you were the guitar player in the group?

J: Once I got the guitar, my other two friends got guitars, and we all learned how to play. I taught myself, and I am left handed, so I picked it up backwards. And I kept wondering why the guy in the picture wasn't holding it like me! I learned to play an entire song backwards before I realized that I had better turn it around. And I didn't even think about it, I just turned it around and learned it the other way, which I think helped me to become ambidextrous.

So, I can say that at that time when I decided to become a singer, my real idol was Janis Joplin. Just for the ferocity of her emotions. This was about 1969.

G: Did you try to sing any of her songs?

J: No, I just admired her and loved listening to her. But I didn't try to imitate her. I have to say that most of my early listening, singing, and heroes were black. That's what I loved, growing up. Although I loved the Beatles, Motown was *it* for me. What great music to grow up with! Then eventually I started listening to Ella Fitzgerald, Aretha Franklin, the blues, and John Coltrane. It has all been black music. I never had a big background in classical music.

G: Did you go to music school eventually?

J: No. I took piano lessons for a couple of years privately when I was probably ten or eleven. I really got a lot from that. In my own career I've learned a lot from listening to other singers and also from asking them how they did things, or how they got their voice to do such and such.

G: Have you found this kind of one-on-one experience valuable?

J: Yes, it's a way to go.

G: There is nothing like getting a private lesson from somebody who is doing it. Then you get focused attention.

J: And you get practical advice.

G: How did you arrive at your present style?

J: Well, I have always listened to music, day and night. Growing up, there was not a lot of music in my house. My parents liked music, but it wasn't a big part of my life. The AM radio was on—at that time in New York AM radio was great. The pop music was pretty good. That's what we listened to along with a lot of Broadway shows—my parents liked Broadway shows. I just found an album, "Mr. Wonderful," which I used to love listening to over and over again.

G: That's Sammy Davis, Jr.

J: Yes. Now, there were a couple of albums that somehow fell into my possession. Magic—that had a big influence on me! I found the albums in the basement, or somewhere, or somebody said, "Listen to this." When I graduated from high school, I asked for a stereo for a present, and I got a little high-fi. I went right to the jazz store in the Village and bought Jimmy Smith and Kenny Burrell. Then these other albums just appeared in my life: Shirley Scott and Joe Newman. Joe Newman, singing—I loved the way he sang. I have always been attracted to singers who are instrumentalists. And an album by a woman named Vi Redd, who was a saxophone player who sang. Vi Redd was an amazing influence on me. She sang a standard called "We'll Be Together Again." In the sheet music you see [Janis sings] "no - tears - no - fears" When she sang it, she made all these notes out of one syllable—she phrased it like she was playing the saxophone. That really had a big influence on me. So when I started listening to jazz, it was more to instrumentalists than singers, I would say. Mostly post-bop, modern stuff. In college I listened to a lot of free jazz, and certainly Coltrane all the time, and Monk. I liked funk and jazz-funk: Eddie Harris, Les McCann: "Compared to What?"—I loved that tune. It wasn't till I met Tim Hauser that I started listening to swing, big band music, and vocal groups like the Modernaires, the Pied Pipers, and the Mel-Tones. I had never heard of them. And then I listened day and night. Chris Connor,

June Christy, and singers with the Stan Kenton Band. I am a student of vocal groups and singers.

G: Do you still listen to them?

J: Oh yeah!

G: Who do you listen to now?

J: Abby Lincoln, "Turtle Dreams"; the soundtrack to "Dead Man Walking"; vocal music from Bali, Indonesia; Cecilia Bartoli, Mozart, Mills Brothers, Ella and Louie, Teddy Wilson with Billie Holiday, Carmen McRae, Sheila Chandra, Annie Di Franco, who I love, Duke Ellington, a Finnish big band, Eddie Palmieri's new album.

G: Do you go through phases of listening to different styles of music?

J: Yes, yes. When I am relaxing at home, like cooking or something, I like to listen to jazz and classical. Some listening I do just to keep up with things—like I bought Joan Osborne's album just to see what it was about. And there was one song that knocked me out, the one about Ray Charles, "I Had a Dream About Ray Charles." Annie Di Franco I bought because I heard her interviewed on the radio and thought she sounded really interesting. She's got her own record label called Righteous Babe. She plays guitar great and she writes very good songs.

G: Do you play piano?

J: Enough to arrange, but I can't play. Now I would love to go back to school—I would love to take piano lessons again. I would just love to play enough so that I could play a few classical things for my own enjoyment. I am very into harmony and always have been. I have always been in groups and have never really been a solo singer. Now I do it just so that I can work with other people and get other perspectives on things.

G: Did you put the Transfer together?

J: No. Timmy and I and Laurel Massé found ourselves together through a series of very freaky coincidences. They had to do with Timmy driving a Manhattan cab and picking Laurel up. And I met him through the cab. I was singing with my group at the time, Laurel Canyon, which was basically the same group I'd had when I was twelve—one girl changed. We were playing and doing really well—we were probably nineteen by then—and I had graduated to a twelve-string guitar. We were just about to get a record deal ourselves. We were singing with Dianne Davidson, from Nashville—more modern country music. We met a lot of great songwriters down in Nashville and I was just starting to incorporate a little bit of jazz into our music.

G: What kind of music did Dianne Davidson sing?

J: Dianne was one of the most amazing singers I ever heard. She knocked my socks off. She was white, blonde-haired, blue-eyed, plump, and she played guitar like nobody's business. She sang like a combination of Etta James and Tracy Nelson—country meets R&B. And I said, "Wow, this girl knocks me out." My group became her back-up group. We sang background for her and we toured with her. We were just about to get a deal on her label, Chess Janus, when I met Tim.

G: In the taxi?

J: Yes—he picked up our conga player, who asked him if he wanted to meet the group. Timmy had heard of our guitar player, Matt Grayden, and he knew of Dianne marginally, and it was an excuse to get out of the cab. So he parked and came up to where we were hanging out, and that's how I met him. He was trying to get himself into the music business again and invited me to sing on a demo he was doing. That session was where I met Laurel. Tim played the banjo at the time, so he would sit in with my group. And then Laurel and Tim and I found ourselves together and Tim was playing all this incredible music for me. He said, "Let's re-form The Manhattan Transfer."

G: So it had existed before?

J: Yes, Tim was one of the original members. It was a group on Capitol Records and they teamed them up with a guy called Gene Pistilli. The album was called "Jukin': The Manhattan Transfer and Gene Pistilli." They were very scattered in their focus. Tim was bringing in all the 40's material; Gene was a very good writer and was writing his own stuff; and there were also other factions wanting to do R&B, so it was really too spread out. I should talk—that's what I liked about it! So, as soon as Tim played me his four- and five-part harmony, I said "This is what I want to do," and I quit my own group. I went back to waitressing and we put the group together.

G: So, it was like a spark that lit up for you?

J: Oh yeah. It was a feeling of knowing. I said, "This is what I want to do."

G: And it has been that way ever since—that's great! Many singers starting out don't know what they want to do, so they're wishy-washy.

J: A lot of people never get that feeling of knowing. It's an act of grace to have it.

G: I have a young student who is bouncing off the walls, not knowing what direction to go in. But he wants a record deal!

J: No, no—that's putting the cart before the horse.

G: Right. So what would you tell someone like that?

J: To focus your ambition. Because you are also entering the business world, where you are going to have to communicate to people in one word or one sentence what you are about. So you are going to have to have a point of view, whether it be your own writing—which would certainly convey, hopefully, who you are—or a style—so you could say, "I'm a hip hop singer" or "I'm a jazz singer." But, you see, then again, I am being a hypocrite. I would never say that about myself. I would just say that I am a singer.

G: But you know inside what you like to sing.

J: Yes, but it happens to be a lot of different things.

G: But in order for you to get where you are, you had to make a decision, and focus.

J: Yes, and when The Manhattan Transfer started, we were focused all the way down to details in what we were wearing—it was very specific. It was a Dali movie—a very surreal scene. We were singing this 40's material with some very complex harmonies, but I remember myself wearing baby clothes a diaper, and I had a big pacifier around my neck and necklaces of baby toys. Eventually we decided on black and white. Al and I wore white and Tim and Laurel wore black. The guys wore tails tuxedos, and Alan had a zoot suit chain and a cane, and Tim had the top hat. Alan and I glittered our lips. And that's how we performed, no matter what style of music we were doing.

G: So you went from 40's to other styles of music?

J: Actually, we started off eclectic. Our first album has gospel, big band, 50's doo-wop. We did "Sweet Talkin' Guy"; we did an Alan Touissaint tune, "A Capella." But somehow it came off focused—I don't know how. I think because the four-part harmony was the thread.

G: That was the thing that was most recognizable.

J: Yes, because at the time, it was a forgotten element of pop music.

G: When did Manhattan Transfer get their deal?

J: 1974, and our first album came out in 1975.

G: What label was it?

J: Atlantic.

G: You're still on it?

J: Yes.

G: So you've had a good relationship with the label?

J: We had a good relationship because Atlantic was one of the few labels where the music lover was still in charge. Ahmet Ertegun and his brother Neshui were in charge of the label when we signed.

G: What do you think of the music industry now?

J: I don't think it's very good.

G: The music lovers have left and the business people are running it.

J: And all they look at is numbers—but there's a big flourishing scene of independents now, so that's always good.

G: What do you think—if Manhattan Transfer were trying to get a deal today, do you think you'd have much difficulty?

J: Yes.

G: Considering all the talent that's there?

J: Well we don't sell any records—I mean in the broader picture.

G: Do you sell more abroad then in the United States?

J: Sometimes we do. We first came across that phenomenon on our second album. We must have sold 50 copies here, and then we got this phone call saying we had a million selling record. "Chanson d'Amour" sold five million copies in France and England. So we went over there and that's when we started making our living there. The second and third albums did great in Europe—England, specifically. We made our living over there for quite a few years.

G: Did you live there?

J: We were thinking about moving there actually. We were there a lot. Then our album "Extensions," which is the first one we did with Cheryl, did great in Japan so we went there and we've been going since 1980 almost every year. Different albums do well in different countries. And "Extensions" didn't do well in Europe. It seemed like people couldn't accept that change from us—they wanted us to be the swing kids or something.

G: Do you have an album out now?

J: We have one out now called "Tonin'" and we're just about to start another one called "Swing." We're really right at the beginning of it, we're still voting on tunes.

G: Did you write any of the material?

J: No, but we're probably going to write some lyrics, since it's a vocalese album and we're basically singing arrangements.

G: We talked earlier about working in groups. How difficult is it to be a part of a group?

J: I think you have to have the right personality and temperament. It involves compromise. It's a lot like being married—except to three people instead of one! When it's right, there's a synergy that makes it better then being alone. It's more powerful, everybody contributes their best self, and what you have in the end product is better then any one person can do.

In a group you can't always get what you want. Sometimes you aren't going to be using every single part of yourself and it might be frustrating—there are always imbalances. Throughout the existence of the group there have been times when not everybody has enough solos, and you sort of have to ride it through till the end of the tour or the next album. There are really some tricks to this interpersonal relationship stuff—to not being trampled on and saying what you want. I've hopefully learned how to really communicate in a way that doesn't alienate my partners. We used to fight in a way that was very detrimental, but now we've learned, through going to a marriage counselor.

G: You guys all went?

J: Yes. We've learned how to talk to each other in a way that makes our fights more productive. Because there's constant conflict. Somebody is always unhappy or maybe somebody doesn't feel good one day and snaps at someone. There's always something, especially when it comes to sensitive issues like who's going to do what solo.

G: Who decides who's doing a solo?

J: Well that's a good question. I've always felt that it's the vocal arranger's call, but the way it's gone around in the group, if somebody brings a tune to the group, chances are they want to sing it—unless they say they heard the song for you, which happens a lot, too. With the kind of music that we do—we do a lot of vocalese—a lot of times it's obvious. Cheryl is really good with clarinets and Alan has a beautiful sort of French horn or trombone timbre to his voice. Timmy does the bass solos. But then you get the tendency of getting locked into things or stereotyping somebody, which is not good. Trumpets are my thing, or alto saxophones. But if I bring a tune in, chances are that I want to sing it, and we learn to say so right in the beginning. On long orchestrated pieces, if I'm the vocal arranger, I'll say up front that this is how I hear it, this is the schematic. "I start off with the trumpet solo, then Timmy comes in, then the clarinet solos," etc.

G: Your group has been together for many years. But you see a lot of groups get together, sing for a year or two and then blow up and disintegrate. A few are successful. What would you recommend they do in order to achieve longevity?

J: First of all, you have to want to stay together; you have to realize the value of staying together. Ideally there should be somewhat of a balance. You shouldn't be in a group where you're doing all the work and you're singing all the leads. The fun really comes in everybody doing what they do best and certainly if you love harmony like I do, you can't sing harmony by yourself unless you're in the studio. There's something very, very spiritual—that's the only word I can think of—in singing harmony. It's realizing your place in the chord and blending with other people, and melding your vibrations into one vibration. It's an incredible feeling—it's a peak experience, I think, in my life. There's something about the sound of voices together in harmony—and even sometimes in dissonance. I think the human being is part predisposed to react to harmonious sound as opposed to dissonance.

G: Have you done any solo albums?

J: I've done four solo albums and numerous projects with other people.

G: Does that create a conflict within the group?

J: Not really, although at some points it has, because it takes time away from the group. I've always tried to do it in between projects. Sometimes there's a fear of what would happen if it really became successful. Are you going to leave?

G: Have you ever encountered bad management or run into any crooks or bad guys in the industry that tried to break up your group? How do you avoid this kind of thing?

J: I don't know if you can avoid it, to tell you the truth. We've been pretty lucky, I've got to say. It's instinct, I think, that keeps you away from these people. We had a manager who was extremely bright and powerful who ended up stealing money from us in a very clever way. We were naive. It was only money, though.

G: But you learned how to do business after that?

J: Well you learn. Mistakes are really a very rough teacher. The other advantage of being in a group is that there are four of you to discuss things, so you have four different points of view. If you have the patience to wade through everybody's point of view, you're going to get a lot of different perspectives. We've made some pretty good decisions.

G: How many managers have you had?

J: We had one when we first started that really couldn't get us a record deal, but we were only with him six to eight months, so it was no big deal. Then we had Bette Midler's manager—Aaron Russo signed us, and he did everything for us.

G: Is he the one who got you the deal?

J: Yes. He actually brought Ahmet Ertegun to Philadelphia to see us at a small club, and Ahmet signed us that night. He had the power to get Ahmet there.

G: So did you play out a lot as a group? Nowadays people don't do that as much—they make a demo instead.

J: No, we played, we played! Little clubs everywhere, bars. We used to play all the time. In those days in New York there were plenty of places to play.

G: And is that how you got your chops together?

J: Yes, that's how we got it together.

G: I know you have a young son—is he going to be part of the music industry?

J: I think it's going to be part of his life and that makes me very happy, because it's brought me such joy. I can already see that he loves it.

G: Talk to me a little about having a young child and touring with him.

J: I didn't have a baby until late in life—I had Gabriel when I was 41 because I've spent most of my life on the road. I've been touring with Gabriel since he was three months old and it's really hard. Of course, I don't want to be without him—I can't be without him. A baby has to be with his mother. And I made the choice not to stop singing. Babies are very malleable, they are adaptable. As long as he's with me it's going to be all right. For me physically it's really hard because I need eight hours sleep and if I don't get enough sleep I lose my voice, my immunity goes down, I'm cranky. With a baby on the road, even with good help, it's really hard. You're always thinking about him and the baby's crying in the middle of the night or in the morning—and you want to go to him. In traveling with the baby, where I would normally have had time for myself, or time to sleep, or play tennis or go to the gym, my time is eaten up mostly by being a mother. When I'm not on stage and working, I want to be with Gabriel. So the time to refresh and replenish yourself is cut down immensely. You've got to have a mate that's willing to share in this.

G: Does your husband tour with you?

J: No, because he's working, too. But we try not to be apart for more than three weeks, or something like that. We're all going to Japan, and then I'm sending Gabe home because I feel it's too vigorous—too much—for him.

G: How long is the tour?

J: It's not so bad—it's only about three and a half weeks, maybe a month. I think it's been a good thing for Gabe—I would certainly rather have him be around my people—my musicians and me than being here in Studio City with some of the mothers at Gymboree.

Our bass player always lets him play drums and he loves it. He loves everybody in the group. He hears all that music every night, he watches the show a little bit. I try and give him good experiences on the road. We've had some good times.

G: You've toured for many years. What's the tour scene like?

J: It's getting harder financially.

G: The tour support isn't there any more?

J: No!

G: So how do you put this together? The label doesn't back you any more?

J: Nope, no tour support. It's hard. You try and get a lot of the promoters to pick up transportation, hotels—that kind of thing. But if you take a day off, it's expensive because you lose money.

G: Is there any advice you could give a singer who's starting out and would like to go into the music industry?

J: I would say that there is no substitute for hard work. I've always been of the mind that you've got to do your homework, listen to everything all the time. I don't think it's a bad idea to really focus and put together a package that says something to people. You have to figure out what it is you want to say—why should I be given the chance to be able to sing to thousands or millions of people? Why would they want to hear me? THIS is why! I think it's good to take every opportunity you can, whether it's a little demo on spec, or singing at a party. Every experience offers something to learn. Certainly getting together with people to jam is fantastic, because in that relaxed atmosphere you come up with things you might not ordinarily come up with. When you're on stage, you're playing it a little bit safe. Also, decide if you really like performing in front of people or not. If you decide you like it, then that's what you should do—go out and perform in front of people. If it's the studio that you like, I think it behooves you to learn everything you can about the studio. You can't have too much knowledge or experience. Try and keep your wits about you and realize that fame is certainly fleeting and the public is very fickle. But the real thing that matters is music and communicating to people. And that's all I have to say!

G: I there anything you'd like to add to this?

J: Singing is one of the greatest things you could do in your life. You couldn't have a better job.

G: Thank you, I appreciate you sharing all this with me and my readers.

ANDY GOLDMARK

Multi-platinum songwriter Andy Goldmark began his career in the music industry as a singer. You may not recognize the name but you'll know him instantly by some of the many songs he has written and the artists who have recorded them: "Soul Provider," "Love Is a Wonderful Thing," and "Save Me," recorded by Michael Bolton, were all million sellers. "Easy Persuasion," "Telegraph Your Love," "Goldmine," Twist My Arm," "Pound, Pound, Pound," "All Systems Go," and "Mercury Rising" were all written for The Pointer Sisters.

Other artists who have recorded his songs are Peabo Bryson, Jermaine Jackson, The Commodores, Jeffrey Osborne ("You Should Be Mine"—the Woo Woo Song), Patti LaBelle, Carly Simon, Jennifer Holiday, Jermaine Stewart, Anne Murray, Lorenzo Lamas, Natalie Cole, Jennifer Rush, Elton John, Celine Dion, Bette Midler, Thelma Houston, Roberta Flack, Appollonia, Alice Cooper, Cheryl Lynn, Gavin Christopher, Al Green, The Stylistics, Peter Cetera/Crystal Bernard ("River North"), Huey Lewis and The News, Kenny G/Peabo Bryson, and many, many more.

In addition to his talent as a gifted songwriter, Andy has produced The Pointer Sisters, Jeffrey Osborne, Carly Simon, Jennifer Holiday, Jermaine Stewart, Natalie Cole, Jennifer Rush/Elton John, and Celine Dion, to name just a few. Now he owns his own record label and is signing artists himself. His vast experience and knowledge of the music industry gives him more than enough insight into what it takes to make it in the music industry.

G: You hire singers to do demos for you. What kind of vocalist do you look for to do demos?

A: I look for a singer who is going to sell the song the best possible way. He or she has to have the right sound, the right range and, equally as important, the right attitude.

G: Is it necessary that they know how to read?

A: Not as long as they are able to quickly learn by ear.

G: How do you find a vocalist for a particular song?

A: Word of mouth in most cases. In the past four or five years, I've found a couple of really strong singers just through the people I work with.

G: So you use the same singers over and over again?

A: I'm always open to new talent, but once I lock in with a singer I like, I tend to go to them first.

G: What would you recommend a new singer do to get started doing demos for songwriters?

A: Make a demo tape that shows off your voice optimally. When you start looking for work, a good place to start is with publishers. Call the creative department and tell them that you're a singer and you're interested in doing demos for songwriters and that you'd like to submit your tape. Give them your tape.

G: What types of songs should their demos contain?

A: Any song that suits your voice, whether it is pop, R&B, country, etc.

G: Do writers take submissions from singers who are trying to break into the business?

A: Sure, all the time. Writers are always on the lookout for the next exciting "voice."

G: Do you allow singers who don't have record deals to record any of your songs? Or do you primarily look for people who are successful?

A: I look for artists that are successful and are going to sell the most records. But on occasion, if a demo singer comes along and says there's a song of mine that they really want to do for themselves, I will let them try it, provided they understand that if an opportunity comes along for me, and they don't have a record deal, I'm going to have to go where the gettin' is good.

G: Are you a singer yourself?

A: Yes, in fact years ago, I was an artist first on Warner Bros. and then later on, A&M. I used to do some of my own demos, but in the last four or five years I've pretty much stopped.

G: Any particular reason why you stopped?

A: Because of the change in music, my voice wasn't sounding contemporary enough and I found a couple of great singers who sing the hell out of my songs.

G: What would you recommend that a singer-songwriter who's trying to get a publishing deal do?

A: The best thing is to pick three or four of your best songs and make a great demo tape, and then use all the contacts you have, whether it be lawyers, managers, friends, producers—whatever, to get you in the publisher's door. Then use all the feedback you get to strengthen your songwriting and demo tape.

G: So you should find out who all the publishing companies are and make appointments with them to show them your songs?

A: Yes, though it's pretty hard to get in the door without a contact. Very few publishers these days will take a cold call and set up an appointment.

G: So how would you go about doing that?

A: There are a lot of ways to do that with a referral from a friend, a lawyer, or anybody connected in some way. How do you begin? You just throw yourself into it, and believe me, one thing will lead to another.

G: OK. Now, is it better to have your own publishing company or sign with a big company? What are the advantages and disadvantages?

A: The advantages of signing with a big company are twofold. When you're young and just starting out, and you need some money and you need some guidance, having a publisher is a great way of getting both. If you're an artist who's young and up and coming, and you signed a label deal and you don't need the money, I would say hang on to your publishing as long as you can because it will become worth more and more as you become more successful. When you're well established and you want to go in for the kill for a big deal, owning your own publishing will make that deal much more lucrative.

G: Is it correct that you just recently started your own record company?

A: Yes, and in the future I hope to have it aligned with a major label.

G: And do you have your own publishing company as well?

A: I have a joint deal with Warner Chappel Music.

G: Tell me how it came about that you started your own record label, because now you're looking for artists yourself, and artists are coming to you for deals.

A: After years of being a songwriter for other companies and artists, and having produced records, I finally decided to take matters into my own hands and make records for my own company. That way, I'm the final decision-maker, without anybody else second-guessing me as to what's going to work best. This is something I'd rather try now than later; at least I'll know at the end of the day where the real blame lies.

G: Have you released your first artist yet?

A: Yes, my first artist is Jennifer Paige. We put out her first single and we got a quick and positive response at radio. It's been a very gratifying learning experience.

G: So are you looking to do more and more artists and become one of those big guys?

A: What I'm going to do with my company is have a major label come in and help me out—distribute and promote nationally. A record takes an enormous amount of manpower and dollars and the majors are the guys that are really best at it. I would love to expand and at some point, perhaps, have a dozen artists I really believe in. In order to become big, I know I've got to start small and grow into the kind of business that can create music, promote it, distribute it, with a kind of class that has made labels like A&M and Innerscope have such impact.

G: What particular style of music would you say is your forte?

A: In the last fifteen years, pop/R&B has been my strong suit. So I love most genres of music. It's the pop and pop/R&B where I feel musically and lyrically the freest.

G: Where did you actually start as an artist?

A: I was living in Connecticut and going to Yale University. I had a second career as a singer/songwriter. During trips I took to New York City, I started knocking on doors of record companies and publishers. I got lucky one day and saw the right A&R person at Warner Brothers, who offered me a deal on the spot after hearing my five-song demo tape.

G: So you've come from being a solo singer/songwriter to owning your own label.

A: Yes. And not in a heartbeat, either.

G: That's a great stat! Thank you very much.

JON JOYCE

Jon Joyce is an acknowledged leader in the session singing community, having a career spanning the last 30 years. His experience reaches back to variety television, where he performed every week as part of the Jimmy Joyce Singers for shows such as "The Smothers Brothers Comedy Hour," "The Red Skelton Show," "Carol Burnett," "The Hollywood Palace," and many others.

Jon has toured with such rock and roll legends as Elton John and Pink Floyd, and recorded with everyone from Frank Sinatra to Linda Ronstadt, Billy Joel and Jackson Brown. He has recently sung (or served as contractor for singers) in movies such as *The Flintstones*, *Apollo 13*, *Jumanji*, *Hercules* and *Air Force One*, among many others. He also contracts singers regularly for TV and radio commercials, Disney vocal projects, and numerous Warner Bros. cartoon projects.

Jon has been a member of the AFTRA local and national boards for many years, where his wife, Susan Boyd, an accomplished singer/performer herself, is currently the Los Angeles Local President.

G: How long have you been a session singer?

J: Seriously, since I was seventeen. I started out doing variety television, and did a lot of that—there were regular groups that did television work. So I sang on shows like "The Smothers Brothers Show" and "The Hollywood Palace."

G: Were you on camera or off?

J: We did both. My session career really started to take off in 1971, 1972.

G: What are the requirements, if any, to become a session singer?

J: There are probably some skill requirements that are difficult to place any firm critical analysis on because taste enters into it. But I think a good ear, a sensitive ear is important. And it helps to have a theoretical knowledge of music.

G: Do you mean reading?

J: Yes, or sort of an organized understanding of chordal relationships, harmonic relationships. You don't have to be a reader but most of the people that I know who aren't readers and who do well have a very well established understanding of chords and whether to sing in the fifth or the third, and can remember those relationships well. Singers who do well as session singers in this business have a variety of backgrounds.

G: What kind of backgrounds, for instance?

J: They usually have a church or college or high school choral background that translates into some contemporary action, whether it be a band or Christian music.

G: That kind of background helps so you're able to sing a lot of different styles of music?

J: Right. You develop a sense of what you sound like and what your voice does in different groupings of singers, and how you fit yourself in. And certainly, recording techniques today have made it possible for singers who are very stylistically oriented or defined to be more successful as session singers than they were twenty years ago. Then there were soloists and there were group singers, and "ne'er the twain shall meet."

G: In other words, if you were a soloist, you just did solos, and if you were a background singer and did section stuff, you were just a section singer?

J: Yes.

G: Do you do solo work now?

J: I do—you could call me a contemporary middle-of-the-road vocalist. I like to be able to say I can do anything from Elton John to Neil Diamond. With a little Leon Redbone thrown in.

G: Are you saying that you duplicate what they do for commercials so you sound like them?

J: I have for TV shows and various things. People want to know that you can change gears. One of the most successful singers in town today—a fellow by the name of Kipp Lennon—started out doing sound-alike source cues for TV shows. He would sound like Sting one week and Paul McCartney the next, and then Michael Jackson—he's a chameleon, you know—he's invaluable. Plus he loves to sing and he has a real joy and a celebration that he brings to music and to a session.

G: How many hours a day do you actually get to sing?

J: Probably less now, because I'm 49 years old and not working as much as I used to. Today—two to three hours a day.

G: What's the most a singer can work per day? Is it an eight-hour-a-day job?

J: I've had many a days that were fourteen or sixteen hours long, where you just went from one session to another. I think if you sing right, the voice stays and what gives out is your back and your feet. Then your mind becomes so soggy that you can't retain anything anymore.

G: What made you decide to become a session singer instead of going for a big record deal and becoming a big superstar?

J: Well, I grew up in a musical family and was surrounded by band musicians and jazz players and singers and people who were not accustomed to their pinnacle of success being a record deal and going out on the road promoting a record. I realized from an early age that that was something that I almost couldn't afford to do.

I know a lot of singers who have had both kinds of careers, and it's a difficult choice to make. If you're having a successful career as a session musician and have a family and have a life—really, it's one of the most gratifying careers you can have, in that you're working for different people all the time, you're working with different singers. Every situation brings a new group of circumstances—different music and rhythm and recording studio and engineer, and all those things. They all form challenges for getting the job done and getting it done well. And it's really exciting! It's wonderful, plus you come home to your family. I have two kids of my own and three stepchildren.

G: What's the most difficult thing about being a session singer?

J: It would probably be the periods of time in between work. Even for the busiest singers, you run into times where you're afraid to ask what's going on.

G: You mean why you're not getting the calls?

J: Yeah—who's working—if *anybody's* working! A lot of times it's just that nobody's working. And sometimes it's just that there aren't any calls that are for you. It just brings out paranoia and every human frailty that you can imagine, every insecurity.

G: Now that we're talking about this, how *do* you get your jobs?

J: Mostly through referral by fellow singers and by producers I've worked for. It's not easy to come to town and not know anybody and try to break into this business. Really, the only way that I suggest someone do this is to associate yourself with songwriters' associations. Meet writers who are in need of singers and do publisher demos.

Usually people who come to Los Angeles from another town as an adult and want to make it in this talent pool have had some experience and some relationships that they have developed in Kansas City or Florida or Boston or Seattle or San Francisco—wherever it was—and often they come with a tape of things that they've done, whether they be local jingles or songs that they've written, or songs that they've recorded for other people.

But those relationships extend out into new areas, because the people you have been working with and for also expand or change *their* work situations. A composer who comes to town who's just a songwriter may get a shot at a TV pilot, and if he has singers that he has used and loves, he calls them. That's how those singers get the experience.

It's very difficult for a singer with very little experience to come to the big producers and the major contractors here in town and expect to get much of a tumble—mostly because you would almost have to be assured of being better than one of those people who are already on the date. So in terms of experience and in terms of what you bring, it's kind of a Catch 22 in that you can't get experience without getting work, and you can't get work without getting experience.

But I don't think it proves to be as impenetrable a problem as some people believe it is. I think it's just a question of some people having the spirit to see through these problems—they always find a path through.

G: You're right about that!

J: I believe that! And I've been here long enough to see the people and almost be able to predict those who come with a spirit that is inquisitive and absorbs information that they translate into their own experience. That's versus other people who knock on doors and expect them to be opened for them and everything to be handed out to them.

But talent is certainly an aspect of this. There are very few people whose talent is so enormous that they are able to "bold" their way into this community. For the most part, it is the ability to assess the skills that are necessary and incorporate them. My wife is a perfect example of this. She came to Los Angeles with a theater background. People who come from a stage background oftentimes really want to stay on the stage—the studio is not a big enough arena for the kind of singing that a Broadway stage demands, plus oftentimes they're not as schooled in vocal techniques and choral singing.

So my wife came into town and she got involved in the jazz group out at Pierce College—it's an ongoing group, but it's a really good training ground for young singers who need an opportunity to sing contemporary music, classical music and jazz vocalese, and to learn to read music. And to meet and establish relationships with other young singers. So it gave her an idea of what was necessary in terms of musicianship skills.

She learned what finesse was necessary to develop a reputation, and her reputation just spread. She had a great rock and roll voice and started out as a soloist, and for years she was typecast as a Linda Ronstadt, a Kim Carnes kind of rock-country voice. But in her heart was a lover of Ella Fitzgerald and jazz standards, and that's what she's doing now. Her specialty is doing sultry jazz standards for commercials and TV. She demoed one of the tunes for Barbra Streisand for Sinatra's "Sinatra Duet."

G: I have the tape she gave me over eight years ago—and some of the jingles on that tape are still playing in commercials!

J: Isn't that interesting?

G: You can have a long life as a session singer doing jingles. If you do a commercial that makes it, you're in and you get those residual checks continuously coming in.

J: Yes.

G: And that's what makes it fun, I guess.

J: That "residual fairy" comes and lives at your house for a while—you're blessed if you can be doing commercials for about fifteen years. The life of a commercial singer is akin to being in the major leagues as a baseball player.

G: Really?

J: Yes—you work long and hard and you're never really guaranteed of getting to that point, but once you do, you're maybe in the leagues for fifteen years—I mean it's very rare that a baseball player makes it twenty years in the major leagues.

G: I've heard it said that there is a little clique of singers that get most of the session work and it's very difficult to break into that circle. Is that true?

J: Well, what I think is true about it is that there are probably a smaller group of singers who are really truly versatile—who can truly astound you with the things that they can do with their voices. Everything from yodeling to doing Johnny Cash to doing Michael Jackson to doing character voices and cartoon voices. They're creative like Robin Williams, you know, and they are very much in demand and you see them often. But I would say that the work today is spread very evenly among as many as 200 singers here in Los Angeles alone.

G: And they go to Chicago and New York and other places?

J: Sometimes yes! Traveling singers. But Chicago has its own talent pool and New York has another talent pool. A lot of this business is "who you know." Very few people are brought into town or brought from out of town—only if a particular client or an agency really has somebody in mind and they demand that that person be used—that's when that happens. But for the most part, we do television here. Los Angeles is a wonderful place to work as a singer because there is a greater variety of work here than there is probably anywhere else in the world.

Japanese producers come to Los Angeles to get their commercials and records done; German producers come here; station packages are done here for all over the world— Romania, Eastern Europe, South Africa.

G: I remember a Japanese producer who came over and wanted me to be a sample for a new Casio keyboard. It was very interesting because I had never thought of doing a session like that—it seemed like an odd session. What's the oddest session you've had to do as a vocalist?

J: The oddest session I've ever had to do was a session for Harry Neilson. He had a song called "The Ivy Covered Walls" which was kind of a lampoon of Ivy League men's choruses, and it was a very sweet ballad that had these very ironic lyrics. He wanted the guys to be very emotional. We recorded for about an hour and a half and there were 24 men at RCA studios (when there were studios at RCA)—and he didn't think we were really getting the point, so he sent out to Martone's Restaurant for pasta and a case of red wine. So everybody ate pasta and drank red wine and then we recorded, and he was convinced, bless his memory, that the difference was audible. And maybe it was—maybe we were a little looser! But we had a fun time.

As far as odd experiences go, I've had some very painful experiences where we took six to eight hours for something that didn't need to take that long, because somebody was on the job who shouldn't have been, you know.

G: They were singing out of tune?

J: Yes, somebody had a girlfriend, and for political reasons you just have to kind of hit the ball and drag Alice, you know—that, or "no relationship." There's no gender reference intended there at all, but it's very difficult to work in circumstances where somebody really is not up to doing something and they don't know enough to bow out.

G: Sure.

J: By coincidence, I just got a call from Shelly Cohen, who used to do all the special material for "The Tonight Show."

G: What do you mean by special material?

J: He put together musical things for Johnny to do with guests, and skits, and he coordinated background singers for guest stars coming on the show—say Vince Gill or somebody—who needed a special group of singers to sing a song or whatever.

G: I always thought the singer hired the background singers.

J: In some cases that is true, especially with larger groups—but oftentimes if I'm asked to put together a group of singers for a producer for a particular project, he or she knows the kinds of material that we're doing and knows singers' types, and thus has an expectation of who I'm going to show up with. So if I bring somebody new—this is getting back to the Catch 22—if I bring somebody new to the party, they better have a bright light shining.

G: They're going to have to deliver?

J: They're going to have to deliver—they're going to have to show some new thing that the person that I have replaced couldn't have brought. That's a challenge.

G: So you have to do more than what's expected, not just what the producer was expecting?

J: Absolutely—you always have to bring something additional, because when they write a rhythm chart out, they have a rough idea of what it's going to be like, but then they want to turn it over to John Robinson and Jimmy Johnson and Paul Jackson or their favorite rhythm section, and they don't expect them to play just those notes they wrote down there. They expect them to bring that special quality that is their talent.

G: Improvise on it? An addition?

J: Exactly—to really make it shine, and that's what singers do, whether they're group singers or soloists. Especially today, a lot of composers are synthesizer and keyboard players and don't write music. So a lot of times they will have a rhythm track and a lyrics sheet, and a rough idea of how the melody goes. They will be asking Philip Ingram or Alex Brown to make this song live.

G: And that's as a session singer, whether they're doing a jingle or a demo for someone or a commercial?

J: Exactly.

G: Have you ever had to sing something you didn't like?

J: Oh yeah, sure!

G: And how did you get into character to do it?

J: Even if it is a silly pop tune, all music that gets recorded has some predecessor—some history, whether it be a Neil Sedaka tune or an old folk song or a children's song—there's an audience there. So in a way you kind of have to figure out what the audience is and sing to it. Whether it's an old hymn for Randy Newman or an Ivy League men's chorus, you have to assume that you know the audience that he's singing to or that he's writing for.

And of course, speaking of Randy Newman, there's no finer person to work for. I worked on the "Faust" album, which is his recent foray into Broadway musicals, and I did a lot of choral work on that. And while it was kind of Gospel tinged, as his stuff is, there was such a sense of humor and wry poking fun at religious tradition! His favorite thing is to kind of get people to laugh at themselves, and it's a joy to be involved in things like that. Then sometimes you turn around and you're just doing silly children's songs for a Disney sing-along video, and then you've got to be pretending that you're singing to your kids.

G: Now, being a session singer, do you ever cross over into doing voice-overs as well?

J: Yes—in fact, the singers' committee at AFTRA and SAG is sponsoring a seminar in May and one of the workshops they're going to have is singing from jingles to voice-overs. What oftentimes happens when you get involved with doing a lot of jingles for one producer, or a couple of busy production houses, is that as a soloist, you'll be asked to do the legal ID at the end. That's where on a beer commercial, for example, you say "Coors Brewery, Boulder, Colorado." Or "batteries not included" or "Member FDIC"—those kinds of things.

G: Do you get more money for that?

J: You should, absolutely. When you're doing the work as an announcer, you get paid as an announcer. There is sometimes the effort to get somebody to do all of it for one fee. But when you're doing the work of an announcer, you get paid for that; when you're doing the work of a group singer, you get paid for that; and if you're doing the work of a soloist, you should get all three payments.

G: What are the average earnings of a session singer?

J: I really don't think I can pin the average earnings. I would say that if a singer was living in Los Angeles and making $50,000 a year, they're in the industry. Of course there are singers who are making less then that—it depends on where you are in terms of your career, too. You know there are people that are not making that much, but they're 22 or 23 years old, just getting their feet wet and just getting experience, working for peanuts. But there are people who make upwards of half a million dollars a year doing commercials.

G: That sounds juicy!

J: It is, and it doesn't happen very often. Those are the Hank Aarons and the Ted Williams.

G: The heavy hitters. So what kind of a demo tape should a person make to submit to producers or contractors?

J: I would say as varied a tape as possible—not over four or five minutes long, and mostly solo material.

G: Thank you very much for sharing your experience with us!

RANDY TOBIN

Randy Tobin is the owner/engineer/producer of Theta Sound Studio, located in Burbank, California. Although the studio was originally created as a means to record his own original songs and compositions, after hearing the results, friends started lining up to book time for their projects and the studio was officially born. In the twenty-plus years that have passed since 1977, Randy has personally engineered and/or produced thousands of projects, many resulting in commercial album releases, as well as film and television themes and scores. Along with songwriter Terry Steele, Randy co-produced the original song demo recording of "Here And Now," which was later covered by Luther Vandross and achieved multi-platinum status.

Being a vocalist himself, Randy knows that capturing the best possible vocal and instrumental performances on tape is the key to reaching the next level in this industry. Although music styles have changed greatly in the last twenty years, creating impact with a musical/vocal message is still what this industry is all about.

G: Would a singer do a better job if he or she knew more about the workings of a studio?

R: Absolutely. When an artist knows what's going on in the production of a project, they are better able to convey their message in the song or spoken word medium. They have more options with which to create, like a painter having special tools and knowing how to use them.

G: What's the difference between getting a good vocal sound in the studio as opposed to on a live gig? And is it easier to get a good sound in the studio than live?

R: Studio and live are two separate animals. The studio gives you a much greater degree of control. That control allows the subtle nuances to be captured on tape or disk. Also, the voice quality will be more perceptible on a recording than live. With live sound, you're competing with other instruments and singers on the stage for optimum volume and clarity. The problem is compounded by the need to be able to move around on stage and still be able to pick up the needed monitor mixes as you move. Live performers also have to deal with other problems like bounce-back, reverberation and blinding lights! So it is easier to get a good sound in the studio because of the control factor covered above. However, the ability to capture that sound along with the emotion and message will depend on the vocalist, the engineer and, if present, the producer.

G: Why does a singer have to sing in a little tiny vocal booth or small space with baffles around them?

R: They usually don't have to. We have the singer in a booth only when a band wants to record the basic or total tracks live and having the singer perform with the band is essential to the ideal feel and groove of the track. Usually this vocal track is used as a "scratch track," knowing that the performer will be redoing the vocals at a later time. When that happens, the new vocals are done in the main room (where there is plenty of space), usually facing the control room glass where eye-contact can be made with the engineer and/or producer.

G: Why it is important for a singer to have one headphone off and one on when they lay their vocals?

R: I actually don't recommend this technique, because music mixes are generally in stereo with different instruments coming out of the left and right sides. Although this can be overridden by the engineer making a mono mix (same mix coming from both sides), it can seem unnatural to the singer. I recommend that singers push the phones back on the ears equally, allowing them to hear themselves both in front and in the phones along with the backing tracks. This is most easily accomplished with open-air headphones like the popular Sennheiser HD-414. If the studio does not have this type of headphone, you may be forced to use the one-side-off technique. If so, ask the engineer for a mono mix.

G: What should a singer listen for when trying to get a good headphone mix?

R: The key is being able to hear enough tracks to be able to sing on pitch while at the same time hearing enough of the live vocal to maintain the pitch. Once the pitch balance is under control, the singer can take attention off the technical factors and put it on the performance.

G: Are some studios better than others for recording vocals, and if so, why? Aren't all studios the same?

R: I think the studio has less to do with it than the engineer and/or producer. I've heard uninspiring results from megabucks studios and some real gems from small project studios. People, not places or fancy equipment, make the difference. Of course, a minimum standard of equipment and its skilled use is important. I wouldn't record a singer on a $10 microphone. However, the first album by the group Boston was recorded with mostly Shure SM-57 microphones (about $100 each these days), and it went multi-platinum.

G: What would be considered extraneous noises a singer makes that would cause problems when doing the final mix?.

R: The most noticeable problem noises are pops and smacks. Pops are caused by blowing air while singing consonants like "P," "B," and "F." We use single and double pop screens to reduce this air flow, but even with these, a hard pop can still cut through. Singers should practice softening these consonants up while singing or by using the technique of turning the head slightly to one side when such consonants appear. Either way, this takes practice. Lip smacks are another problem in the studio. The sensitive microphones capture the desirable and the undesirable nuances. Often, a singer is not aware there is a problem until listening back to a take in the studio. If these noises occur between words or in dead spots on the track, they can be eliminated with today's digital editing systems or automated mixers. However, if they occur within words, the singer must modify his or her technique to reduce or eliminate the noise.

G: What should a singer know when looking for a competent engineer?

R: Most importantly, either the engineer or producer must have a musical ear! It doesn't matter how good you can turn the knobs if you can't help a singer get the best performance. Perfection is not the goal here, the best performance is. But notes that are obviously flat or sharp provide all the reason necessary for a record company executive to stop the tape player and move on to something else. Ask if the session engineer is a musician and preferably, a singer as well.

G: What questions should a singer ask to find out if the engineer/producer knows his business?

R: Regardless of what questions a singer might ask or the engineer might reply, I think the best answer a studio engineer/producer can give is to play you some samples of projects he/she has personally done. Get an appointment to come to the facility and meet the engineer. Talk about your project and ask to listen to examples that are in the same genre. If you cannot personally visit, ask for a cassette with samples of sessions he/she has done. If you like what you hear, you know the engineer is capable of getting the results you're looking for. But keep in mind that no matter how competent the engineer, most of the responsibility lies with you, the singer.

G: What's a good price range for a sound engineer in the studio?

R: Would you pay $20 an hour for a studio that you might take twenty hours to do one vocal in? Or would you pay $100/hour for a studio where you get the result in four hours? This is the question! And since you don't know how long it's going to take, what can you do? Do your homework as outlined above and decide whether more money equals less time. There are places that charge high fees and you must supply your own engineer and/or producer. There may also be some real bargains with talented people in front of the board. One way might be to book two hours in a facility you feel good about and see how it goes. After two hours, you should know if that's where you want to complete the project.

G: What would be the ideal session for you?

R: I like it when singers are prepared and not afraid to tell me that their mix needs adjusting, etc. You'd be surprised how many singers tell you *after* the session they couldn't hear this or that, or everything was too loud! It also helps to be on time and warmed up.

G: What would be the worst situation for you?

R: I've had a few of these and gotten very creative in my approach to handling them. First off, if the singer is terrible, I'll try to get the best possible performance within the reality of the singer, but at the same time, I'll make a decision whether or not to continue after a half-hour or so. If not, I will stop the session and politely suggest the singer get more practice in before trying it again. I don't enjoy getting money for producing unlistenable work. If the session continues for whatever reason, I'll try double-tracking the voice (having the singer sing the same part twice and playing them both back together), as this helps to mask pitch problems. I have had to actually adjust the variable speed on the tape deck while the singer was singing to get a note closer to the ideal. There is a device on the market which digitally corrects bad pitch, but we don't have one in our facility. The bottom line is, what's the use in using every trick in the book getting a recording to sound right if the performer can't come close to that level of quality in a live situation? It really hurts the singer more than helps, and could prematurely end his or her hopes of a singing career.

G: What does a singer need to do to make the session go better for the engineer and the vocalist?

R: Again, be prepared. Know the material. Bring clean, typed copies of the lyrics for yourself, the engineer and/or producer. Communicate what you want to accomplish in the session. Discuss backup vocals and any other parts you think will be added later. Be willing to work as a team to get the best results. Be patient. Don't pressure yourself. Relax. Warm up so you won't go hoarse during the session. Avoid foods that could clog up your system before singing (like dairy products). Get the attitude that you have a message to communicate, and then go for it! The results will be "in the mix" by session end.

You can reach Randy Tobin at Theta Sound Studio by calling 818-9-555-888. You may also take the VIP studio tour on the web at http://www.thetadata.com/thetasound

GORDY GALE

Gordon "Gordy" Gale is the ideal professional soundman to share his expertise in this book because he is not only a soundman but also an accomplished drummer who has performed with artists such as Joe Cocker, Edgar Winter, Danny Wilde (the Rembrandts), Melanie and Bonnie Bramlett. He has worked as both soundman and musician in clubs, amphitheatres and festivals in 46 states in the U.S., as well as in Japan, Italy, Spain, U.K., the Philippines and the Caribbean. His experience as a drummer gives him a realistic viewpoint of exactly what musicians and vocalists experience while performing on stage, and how they can work most productively with a sound person.

Gordy has also worked as a sound tech for numerous music TV programs and award shows in Los Angeles. As sound person, he has worked with Bobby Caldwell, Woody Harrelson, Danny Tate, Chick Corea, Jon Secada, Luis Miguel, Sheila E., Della Reese, Barry White, Terence Trent D'Arby, Little River Band, Pete Droge, John Novello, and myself. I think you will enjoy his honest and straightforward answers and the useful and practical information he shares with us. Please feel free to e-mail Gordy at ggale@juno.com if you have any questions on sound or equipment.

GR: What's the first thing a singer should know to get a good vocal sound?

GG: He or she should know that the sound person will often reproduce the singer's voice as well as possible within the limitations of the equipment he/she has to work with. But sometimes the sound person will tell you the sound is as good as possible when it isn't, because he/she is lazy, or doesn't know how to run the equipment well enough, or is in a bad mood, or for some other reason. So you, as the singer, have to know whether or not you're getting the end result you want, and you have to know how to get it.

GR: What's the biggest problem singers give a sound person at a live gig?

GG: Not knowing what to tell the sound person if they are not happy with the sound. You could say "I don't like how it sounds." But now you both have a problem. My advice is to tell the sound person specifically what you would like to have changed. For instance, "Could you add a little more low end, please?" will get you where you want to be much faster than the first statement, which can come across as a critique.

GR: What should a singer know to make the sound person's job easier?

GG: First, you should really know how to get along with people. Second, you should know what the characteristics of your voice are before you ever get to a gig. The reason is that if there are any voice problems you need help with, such as nasal quality or excessive sibilance, or inadequate volume, you and the sound person can work together to achieve a great vocal sound. And it's just as important to know what you sound like if there are *no* problems to correct, so you and the sound person together can make sure that that sound is duplicated through the sound system.

The third thing you should understand is the basic functions of a home stereo system, such as how to work the bass, treble, balance, and volume controls. Having this familiarity gives a singer an idea of what the sound person is doing.

GR: What's the best thing for a singer to do when there's feedback?

GG: Move the mic away from the source of the feedback. Or, as is sometimes the case, remove your hand from atop the windscreen of the mic.

GR: Most singers don't know the first thing about high, low, and mid-range frequencies. Is it important for a singer become familiar with what these terms mean and why?

GG: Absolutely. These are the fundamental words which describe the general parts of the overall sound. The more familiar the singer is with these terms and their concepts, the more he/she can assist the sound person in working with (mixing) the sound.

GR: Can effects (outboard gear) that are used on a singer's voice in the studio be used on a live gig so the voice sounds the same as the studio?

GG: Yes, generally speaking. However, until you are playing the big time venues, you can expect the effect devices (reverb, delay, etc.) to be of a lower price and quality than found in the recording studio. But this is not always the case, so familiarize yourself with as many of the commonly used effect devices and their sounds as you can. You can even get your studio engineer to write down the effect's settings for you so that you can pass them onto the sound person at the live venue.

GR: What is the most common mistake singers make when they sing and they can't hear themselves?

GG: HOLDING THE MICROPHONE TOO FAR AWAY FROM HIS/HER MOUTH!!! In almost every case, for live sound, for the best sound, as we say, "EAT THE MIC"!

GR: A lot of the younger, hip singers like to grab the mic around the screen and choke the mic. What kind of an effect does it have on the sound?

GG: This technique prevents most of the low end of the voice from going into the microphone, so the sound will be very thin or heavy on the midrange. This is one of the top five things that can create feedback.

GR: What are the five top things that can create feedback?

GG: Although not always the cause, these are some things to check for:

1. A volume knob is all the way up. Solution...turn it down.

2. A slider on the Graphic EQ (equalizer) is boosted too high. Solution...turn it down.

3. A mic is pointed directly into the monitors. Solution...aim it away from the monitors.

4. An EQ knob on the board is all the way up. Solution... turn it down.

5. The PA speakers are positioned behind the microphone. Solution...position the mic behind the speakers. If not possible, play quieter than the loudest that you can get the vocal mic, or learn how to "ring out" a room (which means to use very drastic equalization to compensate for the tendency to feedback).

GR: What is the most important thing a singer should do or know about getting a good live sound?

GG: That the sound person can make or break your gig, so it's in your best interest to find a way to get along with him or her.

GR: What's the best advice you could give a singer?

GG: Be patient. Be professional. Find out as much as you can about every single facet of the music business, including touring, staging, and the technical aspects.

JOHN NOVELLO

John Novello's career spans an unusual diversity of musical accomplishments. As keyboardist, composer, arranger, musical director, and producer, he has played and worked with everybody from Chick Corea, Ritchie Cole, Hubert Laws, Ronnie Laws, Al Vizutti, and Ramsey Lewis to Billy Sheehan and Mr. Big, Edgar Winter, Larry Coryell, Donna Summer, Manhattan Transfer, A Taste Of Honey and Eric Marienthal. As a player he is equally at home with contemporary jazz, R&B, rock, fusion, classical and the avant-garde, and both acoustic and electronic instruments.

A continuing counterpoint to John's professional career has been his love of teaching and helping others on the road to success. With many years of experience teaching keyboards under his belt—which earned him the reputation of being one of the world's most sought-after keyboard instructors—John wrote *The Contemporary Keyboardist*. This manual has become the "bible" of contemporary keyboard instruction worldwide and is endorsed by such top professionals as Herbie Hancock, Chick Corea, Henry Mancini, and Andy Summers. As additions to his *Contemporary Keyboardist* series, John produced *The Contemporary Keyboardist Three Part Video Series* and most recently released a new book called *Stylistic Etudes*, which consists of 86 original song studies that cover over seventeen contemporary styles—jazz, latin, rock, pop, blues, new age, modal, fusion, gospel, country and more.

John has released six solo albums to date and has appeared on many more with artists and groups such as Mark Isham, Manhattan Transfer, Chick Corea, and Mr. Big. He has a new joint CD project in progress with Gloria Rusch that he describes as "scatfunk"—a whole new musical direction and sound. And John's latest project at this writing is Niacin, an exciting collaboration with rock and roll bass legend Billy Sheehan. Niacin is a high-powered rock/funk instrumental super trio featuring John on Hammond B3, Billy Sheehan on bass and the incredible Dennis Chambers on drums. Niacin is currently touring and generating a lot of excitement worldwide.

G: You've been fortunate enough to get that "illusive" record deal a few times.

J: Four record deals to date, and they're always tricky to get and keep.

G: Most singing students who come to me are after an instant record deal. So what I'd like you to do is give an account of what is actually involved in getting a record deal, and what happens when a singer finally gets one.

J: First of all, there's nothing wrong with going in and wanting a record deal—but that should never be the artist's ultimate goal. One should not put *all* his attention on getting a record deal, because all a record deal is, by definition, is a loan of money to the singer or artist plus the services of manufacturing and distribution of the artist's record. So it's no different than applying to get a home loan because you don't have the money to pay for a house yourself! But guess what? In order to get a home loan—or a record deal, you have to qualify!

Now we're getting into the secret of a record deal—qualification. To qualify for a home, you have to come to the table with something, meaning some money down. Then the bank puts the rest down and finances it for you. But they won't finance it for you if they don't think you're a good risk. A good risk from the bank's point of view would, of course, be someone who put a decent amount of money down, had a good credit history, had a stable job, etc. So if all of these qualifications are met, then the bank or lending company decides that you're a good risk and they'll finance your dream home. And of course their exchange, or return, for doing this is the percentage they charge you for the use of their money. If all of this works out, they make a profit and you get your house.

Well, it's the same thing with a record deal. The record company wants to find artists that (a) have developed their craft to a professional level and (b) have something to say that is marketable, meaning exchangeable with an audience. When these factors are present, the record company, as with the home mortgage example, has a chance to be viable, as does the artist.

However, after making sure you have the above assets, *you* need to bring something to the table for the *deal*—in other words, the down payment! The "money down" in this case would be a package/proposal for the record company to review to see if they want to get involved further. This usually consists of a demo of at least three or more songs, pictures, bio/resume, and press clippings that show your activity and history, invitations to some of your live local concerts, and so on.

This, of course, takes some money—some blood, sweat and tears. This is your money down, your dues. And if you really love what you're doing and believe in it in spite of all obstacles, you'll do it. If you're not sure of what you're doing, meaning you have doubts, then this part of the game might be a nightmare. A demo package such as this might take years to finally perfect and it may take $500 or $50,000 depending on the journey—and all journeys are unique. It took Tina Turner over 23 years to really make it. It takes as long as it takes. That's why you must be in love with the *journey* and the *challenge*, and not just the *stardom*!

So the artist is now offered a record deal—the key word here is *deal*. It's a deal—a business agreement—between the record company and the artist. The deal is that the record company (lending institution), having decided after careful scrutiny that the artist in question is talented and focused and commercial enough to invest some money in relative to the potential return in today's market, is going to give the artist X amount of dollars and X amount of tour support and X amount of publicity and promotion to help sell his or her product.

So let's say they give you $200,000. They're banking that you're going to sell at least enough records to pay off the "bank's" investment and do another record and another. So a career can be developed this way—and if we're all competent and a little lucky, the artist might have a hit record! That's what the *deal* really is. The only difference between the mortgage and the record deal is if your record is not successful, you do not necessarily have to pay the record company back if they cancel your contract. They just write it off as a loss and hope to make their money back on another artist.

Of course, if your first record is a loss, then when you make the second, third, and others, you'll have to pay off the loss out of your subsequent records' profits—but not out of your own personal money. And of course, if you don't make money eventually, they'll cancel your deal. They're out the investment they made in you, and you're back on the streets looking for another deal. And another deal may be harder to get now that you've been unsuccessful—but possibly not. It may be a blessing in disguise, because maybe that particular record company really didn't believe in you and you'll now be free to find one that does.

So with all that in mind, you as a singer should first put your attention on getting the technical expertise that's necessary to perform the particular type of music you want to perform. This would mean being able to sing in tune and communicate and have good stage presence and look good.

Second, you should work to develop a focused musical style that has some originality and is marketable—sellable! Nobody wants to hear a bunch of clones, which is why your work should be unique in some way. So at some point a person has to mature and refine their communication and product and come up with a musical direction and style of their own that they believe in.

And third, *after* you've done the above two things, you should put your attention on creating a package/proposal that demonstrates to the various record companies that you are ready—that you have done your homework. Think about it for a minute. If you were in their shoes and you had a company to run, would you sign someone that wasn't ready and didn't seem marketable? The answer, of course, is no!

I said before that getting the record deal should not be the singer's ultimate goal. Of course, you want to get a record deal. But what does that really mean? The singer actually wants his or her voice to be recorded on a CD and released to the public *so the singer can communicate his or her intentions and feelings to the public.*

So what then is the artist's real goal? In my opinion, the real goal is the artist's communication to the audience, whatever that may be—entertainment, a message, a feeling, or whatever. In order to achieve that goal and get that communication across, you need to get the album recorded, manufactured, promoted, distributed and sold to the *correct* audiences all over the world.

So these things are what a person should put their attention on initially. What people usually do is the contrary. I've been guilty of it, and almost everybody I know also has at one time or another—of making the record deal the most important thing. But, as I've learned from experience, doing this can leave you unhappy and really frustrated. Why? When you assign or grant too much importance to what someone else does or may do—in this case the corporate entity called a record company—you assign *them* the responsibility for your happiness and success, when you shouldn't. You tend to move yourself away from being the creator of your own career and think the record company is going to handle it all for you. Wrong! The proper perspective is that the record company and the record deal are but tools that can help *you*, the artist, to create your own career.

G: What should singers be aware of in negotiating a deal? And what happens once you get it?

J: Well, sometimes negotiations break down and no deal happens. Minimize the chances of that occurring by making sure you have a good entertainment attorney. Also, I've seen many artists later get ripped off because they didn't understand certain contractual points. Make sure you understand *everything* in the contract before you sign it!

So the attorneys hammer out a deal and, if all goes well, you sign a contract. That's step one. But step two may take a while, so you have to be patient. By the time you sign the contract, record it and do all the artwork and go over the strategy with the record company and your manager and attorney, and by the time it gets released, it could have taken anywhere from six months to two years! And I have even seen some artists sign the deal and finish recording the record, but then for some reason the record company decided not to release it. This is why you need a good attorney—one who makes sure that a guaranteed release is in the contract, and if the company doesn't release it, then you're free of the deal. The last thing you want is to be tied to a record company that isn't helping you.

So, now that you're signed, a whole new bunch of problems and laws go into play: now you have to get it recorded and released, and then you've got to get some kind of support from your whole administrative team, which consists of the record label, your manager, your attorney, the promoters, the publicist, the critics, etc. This is where the charisma of the artist comes into play. You can't be a VICTIM! You have to sell yourself someway. At meetings, at your live performances, with your charming personality, with your belief in yourself—all of this helps rally your team and pull it together. And believe me, it takes a team effort to launch an artist. I've seen super artist egos kill a project many times!

Getting through step two can be very frustrating, as you still have to make a living while this is occurring. Usually the initial money advance isn't big enough for you to live on for very long. Then, once the record is released, it still takes six months or more for you to get your first financial statement, and if you haven't recouped in sales your initial advance, then you don't get a penny. As I said earlier, you had better love being a creative artist!

G: If you already have all the songs for your record recorded and you take that product to the record company, would that be the demo or could that be the master?

J: Well, there are two ways to get a record deal. One is to just do a demo, which is a facsimile or a prototype of what you do. You put as much money and time and effort into it as you can and you do a three-, four- or five-song demo. If it's really strong and it happens to be exactly what a particular record company wants, then you might not have to go any further. They'll say they want to sign you. They'll hook up with your manager (if you don't have one, *now* is the time to get one), and they'll knock out a particular deal—which as I said, could take three months to a year! Once the deal is knocked out, they put up the money and you redo all the songs—because you want your recording to be of higher quality than the demo.

The other way to get a deal is do everything yourself. If you happen to have your own money or access to a friend or a sponsor or investor, then you may want to risk paying for it yourself. This means you take your own or your investor's money and do the whole record yourself, and then shop the finished master to many record labels and hope you can get a buyer. Each way has its pros and cons.

G: Is that what happened with your last project?

J: Yes, two of my more recent projects. Not my very first project 25 years ago in Pennsylvania, which was done by a famous producer who produced the hit band "Outsiders" back in the late 60s. He just happened to hear us at a club and he signed us just after seeing us perform. That doesn't happen too much nowadays, as mostly if they do see you live and they like you, they still want to hear a demo and pass it around the record label.

But yes, on the deal I just did for the Niacin project, my partner and I produced it ourselves because we didn't want to wait and because we were creating a new music in a new direction. Because record sales are down in all of the stylistic music categories, we knew that trying to launch a new music under these conditions wouldn't be easy. So we decided to produce the whole project ourselves and then we shopped the finished dream to the record companies. This way they either like it or they don't. It's a gamble.

So you see, you can do it yourself, and sometimes when all else fails, meaning nobody wants to sign you, then this option might be your only choice. You could even go so far as to print up 500 or 1,000 of your own CDs, do your own artwork so the record company can really see your dream clearly, and then shop it. But then again, if it doesn't fit their vision, you could get stuck with the CD and be out $40,000 or whatever you put into it. It's your career and risk—and if you believe in yourself, it's what I call a necessary risk.

Having the record company finance the record is in a sense the better way to go, but not always. The down side of it is you can get very frustrated at how long it all takes, and by the time the record company adds their two cents to your vision (and believe me, they will try, since they're putting up the money), your vision may be unrecognizable even to you. Whereas if you do it yourself, things might go more quickly and your vision remains intact. So each of them has their pluses and minuses.

G: Could you go over what happens once you've managed to get that illusive record deal? I've seen you go through many changes, even after getting the deal. I think most singers think that once they get the deal, everything is all set. They're on their way to stardom. "I got a deal now, so I'm fine."

J: Everybody's excited. Great. So now you need to find out how much of a priority you are with your record company. You don't know if you're one of their AA artists, which means they really think you're going to make big money, and they're going to invest a lot of money in you and release and promote your record ASAP. Or if on the contrary, you're one of their experiments, meaning they'll just release you when they get around to it or when they absolutely have to, due to the contract. They'll throw you against the wall and see if you stick!

Many people have this false notion that once you're signed to the label, the label thinks you're God, right? Not necessarily. They may have 50 artists signed. Ten of them may be their AA artists, twenty may be their B artists and ten may be their C, or long-shot, artists. B artists are those that they like enough to put a limited amount of time and money into because they think they can make some money, but not like the AA artists, on whom they think they can make a killing. C artists are those who are either a long-shot or ones they're just not sure of for some reason or other.

So the label puts X amount of money in, and if the first record doesn't work, then they won't pick up your option. Usually the deal is for one record plus options for a few more, but at their discretion. They may have two to five options, depending on the deal. If they don't think you're going to do well after the first record, they may not take your first option and then that DEAL that took so long to make is over, just like that! And that can be the kiss of death because now all the record companies know that your first record didn't do well, which can make them skeptical. Your manager and attorney now might have a harder sell.

It's quite an unpredictable business, but I love it! So if you're an A act, that's great. If you're a B act, that's not as great but it's still okay and better then nothing. And then if you're the

C act, well, good luck, as you may need it. But I have seen C acts make it, too. A Taste Of Honey, the R&B disco group of the late 70s that I was musical director of, is a good example of this. They got signed because some executive at Capitol saw them perform at a wedding. Not many other people really believed in them, as they were a brand new project—two girls singing and playing guitars had never been done before. But he was a top executive and signed them anyway and the rest is history. The tune "Boogie Oogie Oogie" became a huge hit and sold 9,000,000 records worldwide.

So whether you're an A act, a B act, or a C act, any of them can do it—but there are no guarantees. The point here, though, is that you should try and find a home where the record company really believes in you. Most people get so hungry that they want the record deal no matter what! it's a tough decision. But I would also say go for even being a C artist, when all else fails, as getting your project out there is better than not in most cases.

My second deal is a good example of this. I went with a label that didn't have much money or distribution, but who at least were willing to put out my record, which I had produced myself. I was so anxious to get it out there that I went with them. In hindsight I should have waited as it was a good record. It even got a lot of great radio airplay. But the record company did not have good distribution and so they couldn't even get it into the stores in the areas where it was getting airplay. This was not good, because when a customer heard it on the radio and decided to buy it, he couldn't find it at the record stores and then the sale was lost. To this day I wonder what might have happened had I waited for a better label.

G: So distribution is important at this point of the process.

J: Yes, very important! We were number one on many of the radio play lists in various regions, meaning the radio was excited to play it and people were calling up and requesting it. But then they'd go into the store and they couldn't even find the damn record! So there's an example that demonstrates that, just because you get a record deal, you haven't necessarily hit a grand slam. But at least it means stage one of your career—struggling to get signed—is temporarily over.

G: Who are some of the key people a singer or artist should know about in relation to his or her career?

J: Well the *key* people at the record company would be the promotion people. They're the people who are actually going to be on the front lines selling your record.

G: Who do they have to sell it to?

J: They're selling it to retail stores across the country. All the chains, the Tower Records, the Borders, the Blockbusters and all the small mom and pop stores.

So picture owning a store right now. You're trying to make a living and you have all this product coming into your store every week that everybody's hammering on you to buy. So now there's a brand new product that the record company wants to get into your store. Why should you buy Sherry Smith's new album? You don't know anything about Sherry Smith. You look at the package and it's not even on a big label. It's on XYZ Records—a small independent.

Then some promotion guy from XYZ Records calls you up and starts his sales-hype pitch on how Sherry Smith is the next new Madonna, etc. etc. etc. You're overwhelmed with a lot of other CDs you have been sent which aren't selling too well, so you tell the promoter to call you back next week. So that guy keeps hammering on you every week, every week, every week until you finally either tell him no or get it into your store.

Now back to the artist's point of view. Your CD is in some stores. So who's going to know about it? This is where promotion comes in and there are many types. A publicist is usually hired to get you some CD and concert reviews, hopefully positive, in the various music trade magazines. Then there are record company ads that they put in the trades that announce your CD Release. Then, of course, there is radio. The record company sends some promotional CDs to all of the major radio stations, region by region, and hammers on them to add your CD to their playlists. If all goes well, the public starts hearing your CD on the radio and seeing it in the magazines and newspapers, and if they like it, they'll buy it, as long as they can find it in the stores.

A hit would be defined as sort of a run on your record. More and more people start agreeing that they really like this record and wham—you have a hit! Easier said, of course, than done! Or it's not a hit but sells enough for the record company to decide that they'll pick up your option and try another record with you. Then you start the process all over, and write and make another record. But if the record company drops you, then you have to start all over again at step one: getting another record deal. I've seen some artists put out several records and have several different deals before they either find the right label or mature enough to write some material that launches them.

So again, a record deal is not the end; it's only the beginning. You're now on the playing field. You're in the big leagues, and touchdowns and championships don't come very easy. It's easy to get injured—in this case spiritually, mentally, your ego. You could also liken it to buying a McDonald's Franchise. You buy a McDonald's franchise and you pick the wrong location for it. You think that just because you are under the "Golden Arches" of a time-tested hamburger chain, that you're going to be a hit. But it doesn't happen and McDonald's pulls your franchise license. It's because you chose the wrong location. You're right across the street from an Arby's and something else and it just didn't work. So the same thing can happen with your record career. Your project may be ahead of its time—too different, and you chose the wrong label that didn't have the promotional chops to launch this unique project. So getting the deal is only step one.

G: A lot of artists don't know how much money the record companies put into an act other than the recording budget. Could you elaborate on this?

J: Besides the recording budget, a record company has the responsibility of marketing and promoting the record. The production budget is a loan against your royalties. So if they give you $200,000 to produce the record, you owe that back to them out of your profit, should you get any. A normal record deal usually is a partnership between you and the record company that is split up with about ten to fifteen percent (more or less) of the gross sales going to the artist and the rest going to the record company, since they're usually putting up all the money.

For their 85% to 90% they have to not only give you the production budget, but they have to put up money for the marketing and promotional program.

The marketing and promotional program consists of hiring a publicist, independent radio promoters, ads in the trades, buying listening stations at retail record stores for higher profile, tour support to the artist when necessary, etc. This could easily cost as much and more than the production budget. But it doesn't come out of your royalties like the production budget does. The general rule of thumb is that if a record company gives you a production advance of $200,000, then they hope to sell about $200,000 minimally to recoup expenses and make a profit. Anything less starts getting into the red, and too much red and they'll eventually lose interest.

Without this promotion though, other than word of mouth from your live performances, no one will know about you. That's why in record stores you see huge stacks of some artists' CDs displayed very prominently in key locations, displayed at listening stations, etc. The customer is more likely to browse these visible records first and increase sales. Well, the exposure costs money and when it's done, it shows that for now, the label really believes in the artist and is willing to gamble to help break the act. If Sherry Smith is tucked away in some bin in the back of the store, not getting much radio play, and there are minimal ads in the trades, Sherry does not stand a very good chance of success, does she? This is unfortunately the business side of the industry, and an artist should understand this because the more you know, the more causative you can be over your destiny.

G: What about the big picture out in the front of the record store? How do you get that?

J: The big picture out in the front is usually for an established big artist. The record company wants everybody to know that this established artist has a new release. For example, if Sting, who is a huge selling artist, has a new release, chances are that the label and the store are going to prominently promote this fact. This usually means radio ads, big billboards around the city, huge posters at the record store, mega ads in the trades, reviews, etc. A new act hardly ever gets that much from store promotion unless everyone at the record company agrees that you're a double-A act and they can make millions from you. So again, it goes back to this one theme, which is that just because you have the almighty record deal, it doesn't mean it's a slam dunk! The label not only has to believe in you, but it has to have the resources to really help you.

G: They have to really, 100% believe in you?

J: Yes. In hindsight, I believe that if it doesn't seem quite right, it probably ain't. But there's always a solution to every dilemma, and giving up is never the solution. Some artists, for example, shop their project to twenty labels. If everybody passes, they incorrectly conclude that they're no good and they get depressed and eventually give up. Hey—maybe it isn't very good and it needs more work. But even that's no reason to give up! The point here is the 21st label may actually go, "Wow! We've been looking for this." And you won't even believe it! You'll think, "This is insane!" Well, it's not really insane. It's just the competitiveness of the market. Every record company is different and what may not work for one may work for another.

That's why your intention and your goal should not just be to get a record deal, as that's just one target among many you should have. Your goal should be to perform and write and communicate to audiences because you love it. As I've said before, a record company is one tool you can use to realize your dream. Your main focus should always be your singing and getting your vocals together and performing and writing and collaborating with people if that's what you do. Playing in clubs, getting reviews, producing and submitting demos, writing, singing and attacking this like there's no tomorrow is the only way to win and have a good time while doing it. Keep this up and soon you will start producing an effect on people. And once you start causing a ruckus, then you're past the halfway mark. You'll start getting word-of-mouth.

Word of mouth is everything. Good word of mouth says "Wow, that person's really out there, they're persistent, they're always playing. I think I'm going to give them a chance." I don't know of anyone who says "Well gee whiz, I can sing," and then puts a quick little demo together and sends it out to four or five major labels, gets signed and gets released and then becomes a huge star. I really don't! Must be a fiction story that I ain't read yet!

G: Does the artist have a responsibility after the record is released? Some people think now it's just up to the record company.

J: You'd better believe it. As a matter of fact, it *is* your business. The record company, manager, attorney, publicist, promoter should be thought of as your staff—your support team. In a sense, although they are independent contractors, they work for you. And if they're not doing a good job, then get someone who can.

And the artist has a hat, too. He has to show up at record stores to sign autographs and be there for the fans, etc. The record store managers get excited when the artists show up, so they might feature your record more prominently. And then you have to be able to tour and when you do, you have to be good! Because if you do one concert in one city and you're not any good, the word-of-mouth is "Oh, I saw them live and they're not any good!" And then, all of a sudden, wham! There go your sales.

What if you were signed and your record was pretty good in the studio, but you really weren't ready to have a deal because you haven't performed very much? Well you aren't going to cram down overnight something that takes five or ten years to develop, are you? So a lot of record companies won't even let their artists go out when they know they're weak live. They put out two or three records and rely on radio to sell records. And in the meantime, they hire stylistic and vocal coaches to train the artists for an eventual tour.

Technically, I don't think they should even be signed, as there are plenty of talented artists who are good live—but that's another topic altogether. In the 50s, 60s and 70s that never happened, because you had to really be able to sing and/or play to get a deal. There weren't any drum machines and home studios and sequencers and computers.

But now there is so much technology and so much competition that record companies will actually sign someone who just has a good look, an interesting voice, or material written by a famous producer. They think that on these traits alone they can make a success. The advent of electronic technology has made the recording process very easy. So in the hands of amateurs or the inexperienced, records can now be produced. But the standards have really dropped in many cases and the market is flooded with bad and mediocre product.

Once in a while they'll pull it off, but usually it's a one- or two-record act with no longevity. In the long run, doing this is not good for the industry, because the golden age of any industry occurs when people and artists of real talent and integrity are operating. Doing things *only* to make money always seems to backfire. Rather, there seems to have to be a purpose *above* making money to create a highly successful career with longevity.

And you should also realize that your talent by itself is no guarantee of anything. Talent and artistic chops are the basic qualifications that let you in the door. But it's hard work and integrity and persistence that are the main ingredients with which you will create your success.

G: So the correct sequence would be to get your fundamentals together so you can sing and perform both live *and* in the studio?

J: Yes. It's what I call the "Duh! Syndrome." (You know, that sound someone makes when someone says something stupid?) Would you go see a basketball game and stay very long if they couldn't dribble the ball without losing it and rarely made baskets? Hell no! So the same applies to the music industry. Singing out of tune, inability to riff and improvise, bad lyrics, inability to sing and play in tempo—these things are frowned upon.

It used to be common sense. The way this business worked was that you picked a career you liked and seemed to have some natural ability in, even if it was just a little. If it was to be a vocalist/singer, you studied and mastered your craft, either on your own by listening and performing, or by studying with someone. Then you worked your career direction and material, made a demo and shopped it and played live until that big break. If it *never* happened, you still made a living because you were a functioning artist. You had your fundamentals together. You could sing. Duh! Those were and still are the three steps to success: (1) Pick a career and musical direction you really like, from the *heart*. (2) Master your craft. Get competent enough at it to produce the effect that you want. And (3) perform and record and persist until *you* create that big break.

Now if you don't do it this way, you might hit the industry prematurely and have complications, like a premature baby—if it's born too early, you're risking the health of the baby, as it's coming off of the nourishment system. How this applies is if an artist tries to market and shop himself or herself to the industry too early, before their vocal chops are strong, or while their material is weak or unfocused, then their career is at risk.

You actually have to ask yourself why someone would want to do this, anyway? A success oriented individual would or should have this sense. Why would you want to write and perform from a position of weakness? Well, the lure of fame and success is the answer, and if you fall for this, then beware of the results. Premature means "not mature." So if you come out too early, you're either not going to get any deal and get depressed and maybe give up, or if you get lucky and get a deal, it's probably not going to be the right label. You'll be a class C artist and they'll throw you against the wall to see if you'll stick. And if you do, you won't even be ready to get in the race. So that's an unhealthy thing to do.

The lesson here is when your attention goes on the wrong area, all kinds of misfortunes happen. Your attention should be on the excitement of creating your product and sharing it with others, not on fame and money and ego boosting. The way to really do it is to go get a job at a club and perform, perform, perform until you feel great about your performance, pack the place and get standing ovations. Then the club owner calls *you* for a gig and your fans keep asking you if you have a CD out yet, and you start getting good press reviews.

Now you're cooking and have something to manage and present to the industry people. Shortcuts may work but the percentages are against you in the long run. It's not the end of the journey that's fun. It's traveling down the road and developing your act and knowing how much work you've done that gives you this proud sense of accomplishment. In order to get a record deal and have a solid career you have to do the work. Getting famous and rich will be the result. And God help you if you don't know how to stay focused after you get rich and famous. But that's another topic, isn't it?

G: How does a singer find a band? I encounter lots of singers who have trouble doing this.

J: If the singer is not also a musician, it would be probably be best if he or she hooked up with a keyboardist or guitarist or other musician who could act as a musical director. The musical director's job is usually to find qualified musicians and help arrange the material for the singer. Most singers go this way, but some singers are qualified to wear all of the hats. Examples are Prince, Billy Joel, Elton John, Bruce Hornsby, Aretha Franklin, Alanis Morissette, etc. They usually do it all. But I would say that they are the exception. Usually singers concentrate on singing and sometimes writing and lyrics, and therefore they need a band leader or musical director-type support person to help out.

But whether a musical director does it, or the singer or a manager does, somebody has to find qualified musicians. That means looking in the classified sections of the trade magazines for available musicians, looking in the same trades for bands needing a singer, scouring the local clubs for musicians that you like, asking other musicians for referrals (because musicians know other musicians), looking on CDs to see which musicians are playing with which artists. If you have a demo tape and a business card, you can start giving it to select musicians, because you never know, they might remember you and if they like you and your tape, you just might get the audition call. So, I'll say it again—be prepared to deliver if they do call!

In summary, I think a singer should either try to get into an already established grass roots level band so they can get the necessary experience, or start their own band from scratch with the help of another musician.

G: What if you don't have a demo?

J: If you don't have a demo because you've never played with a band, you might be in a Catch 22. So this means you're going to have to find some musician who maybe has a little midi recording studio so you can try and get your voice on tape. If you can't find one, you can just hire a good piano player and go into a commercial studio and do a simple piano/vocal demo. Yes, this costs money, but it's not that expensive. You could probably get a top session pianist for about $100 per tune and find a studio for about $60 per hour. The total cost of the demo would be somewhere between $750 and $1,000. There's absolutely nothing wrong with you saving up your money some way and hiring a musician. There are musicians for hire all over the place—they have to make a living too!

Let's say you don't even have any original material yet. So what? Pick several of your favorite cover tunes and do them. It'll be good experience at the very least and you'll still get the product of your voice on tape. Once you get a good tape, then you can use it to promote yourself. But remember, if the tape isn't good, don't promote yourself prematurely. Go back into the studio at a later date and do another, and another, until you get a good one. Where there's a will, there is a way. Victims don't make it—especially in this industry. And by "victims," I mean people who constantly come up with excuses and reasons why they can't or aren't able to do what's needed and thus don't make any progress toward their supposed career goals.

G: How do good musicians think of singers? Sometimes it seems like musicians and singers don't get along.

J: Often, good musicians only respect singers who literally instantly blow them away. The reason for this is it usually takes a long time and a lot of dues to become a great musician, so if a singer comes along who doesn't know the craft, the musician figures that singer better be damn good! This means they don't have an intonation problem, they have great phrasing, can riff and improvise, are focused and have good stage presence. If you can't do all that—and most singers can't initially, because they have to take time to develop that—then most musicians won't think that highly of them.

Also, in general, more musicians are trained than singers, so this contributes to the communication breakdown and is where that attitude comes from. It can seem to become "the singer versus the band." And this will manifest itself in a variety of ways—the musicians will play too loud behind you, not be willing to transpose your song to the key that's best for you, wince behind your back when you're out of tune, and so on.

Now that doesn't mean that doing that is okay. It means musicians themselves are a little immature, because real professionals shouldn't be like that. It's all normal amateur behavior that a lot of people tend to exhibit before they become successful professionals. And unfortunately, singers will have to deal with it. But then again, if you're a new singer, you are probably not going to be hanging out with the top notch professional musicians anyway. More likely you're going to be hanging out with musicians who are themselves just learning the ropes.

So unless you're a singer who is one of the best around and has some musical tech, there's always going to be a little of the musician/singer syndrome that you're just going to have to deal with. That's why it is good to have some sort of musical director friend/collaborator to help you. But the best way around it is to really become a good singer and don't give them any reason to be critical of you. Just blow them away! Musicians will then want to please you, because everybody knows that a hit singer can really be a big star and that means money and fame and tours.

It also wouldn't hurt to get some musical training. If you can demonstrate to a musician that you can play a little and you know some theory, and what a key is, and time, and chords, and so on, you'll get instant respect because you're now speaking their language. Imagine when a singer turns around to a musician and says, "Hey, that's the key of F. I told you my key is a whole step lower, E flat. Could you please transpose it to E flat? And oh, by the way, you guys are rushing a little. I need it a little slower so it grooves better—say about a quarter note = 78. Thanks!" Yikes! They'll about have a religious experience, as usually this is not the case. Now they're thinking, "Here's somebody that knows what they're doing. We better be on our toes!" So if you get some training it never hurts—and it doesn't take much. This is why I tell singers that, although it's not absolutely necessary, getting some training always helps. It makes you less of a victim and can shorten your runway to success. So good luck!

G: Thanks!

CHAPTER 11

NOW I'M A STAR! WHERE DO I GO FROM HERE?

You have lots of money and recognition and what looks like a great future. If you've really been on top of things and taken care of your business prior to your rise to stardom, then you're in a pretty good position. On the other hand, if you took your advance and went on a major spending spree—ran out and bought cars, a new house, treated all your friends to parties and shopped until you dropped—you may be in for a rude awakening. Unfortunately, that is often what has happened with the "one-hit artist" you never hear from again.

If you've paid off *all* of your past debts—everyone you can possibly think of you owed money to—and invested the remainder in things you know will help forward the future progress of your career, then you've been very wise.

You probably have a manager, agent and lawyer. You should also find a good and honest **business manager**. A business manager is someone who is responsible for taking care of your financial obligations, investments, bills, etc. Before you just give your power of attorney to just anyone, get references and interview each business management company you are considering working with to see what services they offer and if you feel safe sending all your money to them to disburse.

As I've said before, the music business is a business, and you should treat it like one. After all, it's how you earn your living, even if it is a lot of fun. The record companies know it's a business—that's why they are so picky when it comes to signing artists. They just want to make sure they are going to be able to sell records. Can you blame them?

If you want to make sure you are going to be able to continue selling records past your first hit, you had better keep on top of things artistically, too. You should continue to do the successful things that got you where you are. Stay in touch with the people who've helped you become successful. At the same time, find new ways to expand, whether it be finding new writers to collaborate with, or getting into new areas so that you're continually growing. The record labels do this by putting together two successful artists to create a new sound.

As time permits, explore other areas of the arts you might want to get into. Whitney Houston started her own motion picture production company and began acting. Maria Carey is starting her own record label. Michael Jackson has his own label. Babyface writes for and produces other artists and has his own label. If you don't have the expertise to start your own label, find someone you know who can and form a partnership. Continue to make records, but when you are certain you are financially secure, which may take a few years, expand into other areas. Maybe it's been your dream to play the stock market, buy gold, property, or own a restaurant. Whatever you do, make sure you causatively create your future. Keep in mind that the music scene is always changing. New faces and sounds come along everyday, so you have to stay on top of things if you want to survive.

There are many, many artists who sold millions of records but were careless with their money and are broke now. It's very tempting to just run off and play, once you've made it. I'm not saying you can't have fun and play and spend some of your money, but you have to take care of business. Hire professional business people who know what to do with money to make it work for you.

Also, consider getting trained in financial business management yourself so you'll know whether or not something that someone tells you is correct—or you're being cheated! Most artists don't want to bother with the business side of the business, but that's a *big* mistake. Both my husband and I have done courses on administrative and financial management. Now when we have to discuss things in that area with the financial people who work with us, we can do so intelligently and on an informed basis. You'll never be cheated if you understand the mechanics of how finance and business administration work. Get trained and involved in the business and you'll be successful!

EXERCISES

1. Check yourself! Have you set up your business so that you will benefit from all your hard work?

2. If you don't have a business manager yet, find one fast!

3. Find another way to expand yourself artistically.

CHAPTER 12

THAT'S ALL FOR NOW...

Working in the music business is a wonderful and exciting way to live your life, in spite of the villains you occasionally run into. There *are* more good guys than bad guys! If you are true to your goals and really work hard, then you'll succeed. There is one thing that almost every successful musician and artist has said about their decision to make it. At some point they had to make the decision to "go for it" at all costs. They spent their last dollar getting their demo made or doing a photo session. They didn't know how they were going to pay rent or make their car payment and had to live off of TV dinners. But they kept on believing in themselves and what they wanted to do. Things will get really tough sometimes, but if you believe, and never give up, you'll make it.

Thus, if you were to ask me, "When do you decide that it's not going to work and it's time to give up?" my answer would be: "When you don't have any more breath left in your body!"

It looks like that's all I have to say about this subject for now! I hope I've given you enough information about this small part of the music industry to help you make some sane and intelligent decisions about your future. I have told you everything I know about starting a career as a professional singer and succeeding at it. I'm not saying I know everything there is to know, though, because I'm still finding more out about the business myself—things are constantly changing in this industry. You, too, should always keep your eyes and ears open so you can take advantage of changes and new directions, no matter what stage of your career you've reached.

If you still have questions, you can reach me by internet, e-mail, U.S. Mail, or by phone or fax. My addresses and numbers are below. I'd like to hear from you! Until then, good luck with your career.

Worldwide Web: http://www.primenet.com/~rusch

E-mail: rusch@primenet.com

Telephone: (800) 60-VOCAL – Fax: (818) 506-5559

U.S. Mail: Ron Moss Mgmt., 2635 Griffith Park Blvd., Los Angeles, CA 90039

BIBLIOGRAPHY

The Voice of the Mind, by E. Herbert-Caesari (Alma and Rolf Gramatke, London NW6 7QS, 41 Mowbray Road, United Kingdom, Ninth Printing, 1996). (Available through Gloria Rusch.)

Tradition and Gigli, by E. Herbert-Caesari (Alma and Rolf Gramatke, London NW6 7QS, 41 Mowbray Road, United Kingdom, 1996). (Available through Gloria Rusch.)

The Science and Sensations of Vocal Tone, by E. Herbert-Caesari (J.M. Dent, Ltd., London, 1977). Addenda, page 177. (Out of print.)

The Alchemy of Voice, by E. Herbert-Caesari (first published in Great Britain in 1965 by Robert Hale Limited, 63 Old Brompton road, London S.W. 7.; printed by Ebenezer Baylis and Son, Ltd., The Trinity Press, Worcester and London). (Out of print).

Vocal Truth, by E. Herbert-Caseari (Crescendo Publishing, 132 West 22nd Street, New York, New York 10011, U.S.A., 1969). (Out of print.)

Note: I suggest that a book finder be used to locate the three Herbert-Caesari books listed above that are out of print. Or check a library that has a very large selection of books on singing or has a section dedicated to art. A good example is the Brand Library in Glendale, California, U.S.A.

The Contemporary Keyboardist, by John Novello (Warner Brothers Publications Inc., 15800 N.W. 48th Ave., Miami, Florida 33014 U.S.A., 1986).

Art, by L. Ron Hubbard (Bridge Publications, Inc., Los Angeles, California, U.S.A., 1991).

Life Is a Contact Sport: Ten Great Career Strategies That Work, by Ken Kragen with Jefferson Graham (William Morrow and Company, Inc., 1350 Avenue of the Americas, New York, New York 10019 U.S.A., 1994).

Dreams into Action, by Milton Katselas (Dove Books, 301 North Cañon Drive, Beverly Hills, California 90210, U.S.A., 1996).

This Business of Music, by Sidney Shemel and M. William Krasilovsky (Billboard Directories, U.S.A., 1995).

More About the Business of Music, by Sidney Shemel and M. William Krasilovsky (Billboard Directories, U.S.A., 1994).

Hit Men: Power Brokers and Fast Money Inside the Music Business, by Frederick Dannen (Random House, Inc., New York, New York, U.S.A., 1991).

Fresh Vegetable and Fruit Juices, by N.W. Walker D.Sc. (N.W. Walker, Sullivan Woodside & Company, 2218 East Magnolia, Phoenix, Arizona 85034, U.S.A., 1936).

Your Body's Many Cries for Water, by F. Batmaghelidj, M.D. (F. Batmaghelidj, M.D, Global Health Solutions, Inc., 2146 Kings Garden Way, Falls Church, Virginia 22043, U.S.A., 1992).

Enter the Zone, by Barry Sears. Ph.D. (Harper Collins Publishers, Inc., 10 East 53rd Street, New York, New York 10022 U.S.A., 1995).

40-30-30 Fat Burning Nutrition, by Joyce and Gene Daoust (Wharton Publishing, Del Mar, California, U.S.A., 1996).

Practice Hours Daily

Total Hours for the Week _____

Practice Hours Daily

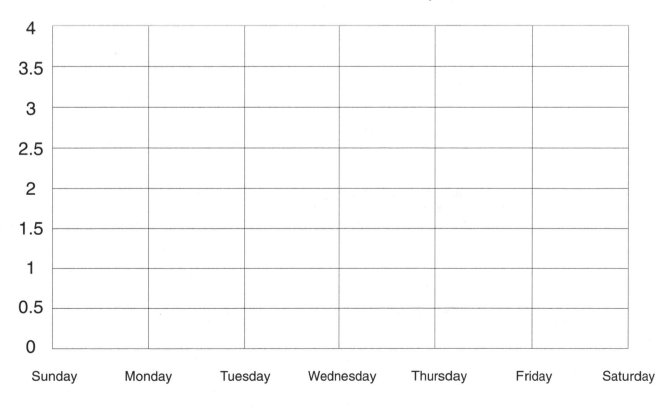

Total Hours for the Week _____

Vocal Exercise Tapes

Caesari Vocalises
3 Volume Set
containing 12 cassettes
with over 50 exercises!

What are the Caesari Vocalises? (pronounced chez-ah-REE vo-kah-LEE-zeez)

These powerful and comprehensive exercises will help any singer in any style **improve** his or her **voice** and **have better control**. With them you can **increase stamina, strength, flexibility** and **extend your range**. Special exercises are included to develop the middle voice and correct specific problem areas such as **breath control, straining** and **sore throats**. Using the Caesari Vocalises will **prevent vocal nodes** and **restore a failing voice**. In addition, these exercises develop the abilities needed for **improvising, singing intervals** and **solving pitch problems**. The professional singer will have extraordinary control and vocal freedom after mastering all three volumes. Each set comes with a complete instruction booklet.

The Caesari Vocalises are a convenient way to warm up before a concert, recording session, on tour or between lessons.

What students are saying about these tapes:

"I can't tell you how much (Gloria) and the Vocalises have helped me! I have much more control over my voice and as a result, more control over my performance as a whole." C.S.

"This is the most complete package of lessons I've ever encountered. These lessons have given me better pitch, more range, confidence, tone, discipline and emotion. Basically, the tapes have changed my life and my voice." B.B.

Special price for the 3 volume set only $129.95! ORDER YOURS NOW!

Name _____

Address _____

City_____ State___ Zip _____

Phone _____

Payment ☐ Check ☐ Visa ☐ MasterCard ☐ Amex

Card Number _____

Expiration_____ Signature _____

ITEM	QTY	PRICE	AMOUNT
Caesari Vocalises 3 volume set		$ 129.95	
Caesari Vocalises volume 1 only		49.95	
Caesari Vocalises volume 2 only		49.95	
Caesari Vocalises volume 3 only		49.95	
Calif. residents add 8.25% sales tax			
Shipping within the U.S.			10.00
		TOTAL	
Make checks payable to: Rusch Productions, 11726 La Maida St.,			
Studio City, CA 91607. (800) 60-VOCAL Allow 2 weeks for delivery.			